IMMEMORIAL SILENCE

Karmen MacKendrick

STATE UNIVERSITY OF NEW YORK PRESS

cover art: Second Version of Triptych (left panel), by Francis Bacon (1909-1992). Copyright ARS, NY. Reprinted by permission of the Tate Gallery, London, Great Britain.

Published by
STATE UNIVERSITY OF NEW YORK PRESS
ALBANY

© 2001 State University of New York

For information, address
State University of New York Press,
90 State Street, Suite 700, Albany, NY 12207

Production and book design, Laurie Searl
Marketing, Fran Keneston

Library of Congress Cataloging-in-Publication Data

MacKendrick, Karmen, 1962–
  Immemorial silence / Karmen MacKendrick.
    p. cm.
  Includes bibliographical references and index.
  ISBN 0-7914-4877-0 (alk. paper) — ISBN 0-7914-4878-9 (pbk. : alk. paper)
    1. Silence (Philosophy) 2. Language and languages—Philosophy. 3. Time. 4. Eternity.
  I. Title.

BD360 .M33 2001
110—dc21

00-036568

10 9 8 7 6 5 4 3 2 1

IMMEMORIAL
SILENCE

Why yet another book, where a seismic shuddering—one of the forms of the disaster—lays waste to it? Because the order of the book is required by what the book does not contain—by the absence which eludes the book.

—Maurice Blanchot, *The writing of the disaster*

Contents

$\mathcal{A}$cknowledgments

I must, of course, accept first and final responsibility for this odd and flawed little book. But a number of others have assisted in bringing it to being, or improving it here and there, or simply helping me to maintain during the writing process what sanity I possess.

In the first category I must thank Boris Belay, who has the wholly unnerving habit of calmly informing me that I have been scheduled to speak on topics for which I am fundamentally unqualified (or at least unready). Though frightening, this has often proven productive. My thanks, too, to those who have invited me to speak in lectures or permitted me to participate in conferences in which I was able to develop this material—including members of the Department of Comparative Literature at SUNY Buffalo, the School of European Studies at the University of Sussex, the School of Humanities at Penn State Harrisburg, the Department of English at Lakehead University, and the Society for Phenomenology and Existential Philosophy.

Among those who have improved this work through conversation, suggestion, and the provision of references I am grateful to Bruce Milem, who is always thoughtful and helpful, besides being almost frighteningly well-read. Peter Manchester's kind and helpful enthusiasm for my ideas dates back to the courses I took with him as a grad student. Richard Armstrong, my endlessly enlightening source in classics, has managed never to make me feel stupid no matter how basic my inquiries. Joanna Crosby, as an outside reader, offered sound and helpful suggestions. Professor David Biale has been both gracious and generous in providing me with references.

For intellectual and personal support I owe still more debts. Crispin Sartwell has exhibited a wonderful faith in this book, often exceeding my own. Most of the text was written while I was a member of the philosophy department at Gettysburg College, and my colleagues there—Lisa Portmess, Kerry Walters, and Johannes Bulhof—were persistently supportive and encouraging, if occasionally a bit bewildered. Alex Caswell, by his enthusiastic reading and discussion of the manuscript, reinforced my faltering faith in its intelligibility.

Jane Bunker, SUNY's deceptively gentle philosophy editor, has been a stubborn supporter of this project from the beginning. It would never have neared print without her. And I am delighted to have again the privilege of working with production editor Laurie Searl, whose visual intelligence is matched by her calm patience with scatterbrained authors. I am grateful as well to Ramin Ashraf, who always finds the perfect cover art.

And finally, to the group of friends who remain convinced of my intelligence and ability without ever demanding anything so vulgar as evidence, I once more extend my endless appreciation.

introduction

*W*hen to keep silence?

prefatory note: tangling the lines

> We set up a word at the point at which our ignorance begins, at
> which we can see no further.
> —Friedrich Nietzsche

Some years before beginning this introduction, I finished writing my doctoral dissertation. Contrary to both protocol and expectation, I had enjoyed the process—perhaps because I had chosen to write about desire and pleasure. (I still sometimes make the rather feeble joke that this allowed me to justify all of my recreational activities as research.) Because I was most interested in pleasure and desire at that pitch of intensity at which they become wonderfully strange, I focused on examples from art, sex, and religion. I found and still find this trio curiously difficult to disentangle. Among the most interesting and intellectually fruitful of pleasure's peculiarities was that of the temporality of the pleasure-desire pairing. The work's central chapter, accordingly, dealt with time.

Its two-page preface was about silence.

I did not have anything in particular to say about silence, but it seemed to me that as I attempted to explore the paradox of pleasure in relation to desire, I continually encountered points of silence, and, in fact, discourse about silence—though more often with regard to religious than to erotic or artistic pleasures. Some connection between silence and intensity threatened to emerge there. In the present work, I think, it finally does.

I knew as I wrote it that the dissertation would not become a book but would provide me with material to develop into several further works. It was always my intention, however, to make the discussion of time the last of these, which I assumed meant that I had more than a decade before I would

1

have to confront the subject again. This optimistic intention was based not on some well thought-out plan, but on a sort of fear. There is something quite terrifying about temporality itself, even in theory, and my hope was that the intervening time I envisioned would permit me the development of sufficient theoretical sophistication to see that, and why, this fear was misplaced. But I have also found that some significant component of writing is nonvoluntaristic, and rather sooner than I had expected it was time to deal with time.

It became time because I finally understood the approach that the work on time demanded. Certainly I was not particularly interested in a metaphysical discussion. This disinterest was due less to any conviction regarding the demise of metaphysics than to a sense that these concerns were at too great a remove from my founding fascination with desire. (I suspect, too, that the "death of metaphysics" remains an intractably metaphysical concern.) Nor did I want to take an experiential—psychological or phenomenological—approach, knowing not only that others had done such work better than I could, but also that something about which I wanted to speak was missing there. It took only a little longer to realize that speaking, loosely speaking—that is, language both spoken and written—was the other axis of the questions demanding to be asked. The relations of silence to language mirror the equally complex set of relations between time and eternity, and it was this fourfold entanglement that called to my thinking.

More precisely, my concerns in this work may be placed along two axes. The first, deriving from a concern with language and its limits, is that of language and silence. The second is that of time and eternity, specifically of the temporality and atemporality of language and of silence. In the following chapters I shall explore this series of intersections through the work of authors in philosophy, in literature, and in religion, where eternity and silence have long been matters of concern.

theoretical silence

> They will then understand why my mind is not all here; then they will see all language go dry, all minds parched, all tongues shriveled up.
>
> —Antonin Artaud

Contemporary theory throughout the humanities is reflexively concerned with its own limits. To some, this is a concern with the boundaries of thought itself—and with what goes beyond or lies outside of thought, in the tradition of Maurice Blanchot's "outside," or Georges Bataille's "non-knowledge." For others (the options are obviously not exclusive) this concern is with the limits of language. Here the entanglements quickly emerge. One of the things that language invariably manifests is time; language cannot be atemporal, so, as Blanchot says of silence, it cannot be kept safe from the passage of time. Thought and language are, at the very least, quite difficult to disentangle; we cannot speak outside time as we cannot think outside time. Kant may well have been right to see time as the mark of all experience of the subject.[1] Nor can we pinpoint one of these impossibilities as originary or causal; in the beginning of our philosophy is the word.

The concern with the limits of language is a tradition with multiple roots: we find it in ancient mysticism as the "ineffable," in negative theology as the unnamable, in the Nietzschean warning that grammar seduces us into a belief in metaphysics, even in the Wittgensteinian warning that philosophy, being all language games, must not infrequently remain silent.

"Whereof one cannot speak," Wittgenstein sternly warns in the *Tractatus*, "thereof one must be silent."[2] Despite the impossibility of keeping his order, we might say that Wittgenstein was right, in the sense not merely of the possible but of the imperative. Some things are destroyed in the speaking, already lost in any translation. As Michael Sells points out in his work on apophatic theology, "[A]pophasis is not the only discourse that cannot directly name its subject. Poetry, drama—almost any form of art—risks being trivialized when its meaning is defined and paraphrased discursively."[3] But we might note further that the loss inherent in speaking is silence itself. And in the more deeply hidden loss of writing (caught up, as Blanchot also argues, in repetition) is silence again.

Whatever respect we might have in theory for the Wittgensteinian imperative, we seldom truly grant, to ourselves or others, the right to silence. We permit it in our law when we already face the possibility of condemnation: on your own behalf, you may remain silent. But you have the right to an attorney: someone else will speak for you. You may be silent, but there will not be silence. Silence is damning, we think. Yet I shall argue that the notion of redemption, if it retains any sense for us, is manifest within language where it is fragmented by silence. As Louis Mackey writes in his exploration of Augustine's *Confessions*, "Language can redeem as well as destroy; it redeems when the Word itself speaks in the silence of our words."[4]

Although the limits of philosophical and, more broadly, theoretical language are certainly of contemporary concern, the admixture of theological

issues I adduce here may seem less contemporary. My intention is not to argue
for a new mysticism, though we must acknowledge that within Western religious traditions we have largely granted silence to the religious mystics, who
are or claim to have been transported to the ineffable. This may be due to the
relative rarity of such experience; not having been there ourselves, we may
accept our inability, and that of our language, to understand. This acceptance, however, is not what it once was. Perhaps mysticism seems so odd or
archaic to us because it has no place in a fully confessional culture. Many of
us scoff at the ineffable, at the very possibility of ineffability, and assume that
whereof one cannot speak, one is simply inadequately educated and articulate—or lying. I would suggest, however, that matters are more complex: that
within even the most articulate speaking there murmurs the loss of meaning,
the coming of the absence which is silence. Religious preoccupation arises
here as one aspect of the preoccupation with a/temporalities of language and
silence; religious thought, too, is the traditional locus of concern with eternity. And so when we take up together the concerns of language and time at
their limits, religious thought is an obvious source.

Religion, however, is not the only locus of thoughts of ec-stasis. As others have noted, we used to grant the right of silence to seduction, perhaps
until we became too democratic or simply too capitalistic. Seduction, says
Jean Baudrillard, is an aristocratic preoccupation, as opposed to "the bour-
geois era [which] dedicated itself to nature and production."[5] We have never
granted it to sex, demanding (pruriently or clinically or morally or sociologi-
cally) that everything be said, that everyone tell all. "Eroticism," says
Bataille, "is silence; . . . it is solitude. But not for people whose very presence
in the world is a pure denial of silence, a chattering, a neglect of potential
solitude."[6] Eroticism in Bataillean terms shares with religion an excessive
economy, an intensification beyond meaning, a transgression of the very
boundaries of speaking, of writing, of language, and of time.

The pornographic strategy, says Baudrillard, which undermines the
power-undermining pleasures of seduction, exists only "in a culture that
makes everything speak, everything babble, everything climax."[7] Everything
must be said; it must be said *now*, with nothing left out—it has to *get* somewhere. Our sense of the sacred has been reduced to sociality and law, our
sense of the erotic to the pornographic and self-evident.

That these issues belong together may not be obvious. Yet our sense of
redemption in post-Nietzschean theory (that is, after philosophers face the
proposition that God is dead) is as much erotic as sacred, and as much disas-
trous as quiet. In the atemporality of silence within language, we find redemption not in an eternal presence, but in the complications of silence and

absence. Perhaps, as T. S. Eliot, a poet much concerned with both time and redemption, writes, "If all time is eternally present,/ All time is unredeemable."[8]

These complications of time by eternity and language by silence are never easy to grasp. Silence is slippery; it shares a double elusiveness with language, for neither will permit of keeping. After all, if we so much as say *silence*, we have already destroyed it. Bataille writes, "I will give only one example of a 'slipping' *word*. I say *word*: it could just as well be the sentence into which one inserts the word, but I limit myself to the word silence. It is already . . . the abolition of the sound which the word is; among all words it is the most perverse, or the most poetic: it is the token of its own death."[9] We can only approach silence, indicating where it would be, if we could say it. This too echoes the apophatic approach in theology. Denys Turner writes, "[T]he apophatic is what is achieved, whether by means of affirmative or by means of negative discourse, when language *breaks down*. The apophatic is the recognition of how this 'silence' lies, as it were, all around the perimeter of language . . ."[10]

This indirection is nonetheless philosophical. It is fashionable to say that we have come to the end of philosophy, but this is nonsense, though it may be that the boundaries of philosophy are increasingly fluid and permeable. Emmanuel Levinas writes,

> Blanchot does not see, in philosophy, the ultimate possibility; nor, as a matter of fact, does he see in possibility itself—the 'I can'—the limit of the human. Everyone seems to think this century is the end of philosophy! This includes those who want to build a better world, to bring about change, and not just understand, as well as those who, at the other end of the spectrum, go back to the "truth of being" with Heidegger. . . . Contemporary thought holds the surprise for us of an atheism that is not humanist. The gods are dead or withdrawn from the world; concrete, even rational man does not contain the universe.[11]

Silence and eternity slip beyond the containment of words in time. We still must use words; we still must draw out the questions that lie within philosophy. It is only that we have learned that we must use philosophy against itself, wrap our words around spaces without words, and leave them wordless, as if they could thus be kept, though we know that we lose them together with ourselves.

The ideas of loss and slipping imply, too, the *passage* that is perhaps the most pronounced characteristic of time. The idea of eternity, in complex relation to time, is itself linked to the "outside," the mystical, the intensified. But if time is intensified in eternity, then we must understand temporal loss even within eternal presence. The relations of time to eternity do not in any simple way mirror those between language and silence but are already caught up within them. The relation of language to time is not simply the creation of an impression, possibly illusory, of endurance through temporal change (of this, more below). Languages are tensed: to speak or to write is always to speak or write at a time and of a time, to imply some relation between the time of speaking or writing and the time of that of which one speaks or writes. We are unsatisfyingly incapable of atemporal saying, as St. Anselm long ago indicated in his effort to give tense to God: "You were not, therefore, yesterday, nor will You be tomorrow, but yesterday and today and tomorrow You *are.*"[12] The poet Edmond Jabès gives us the more painful obverse of this eternity in his evocation of return: "*Yesterday and tomorrow are curves of the same infernal round for you, and your bounds out of bounds so many wounds in their pain. . . .*"[13]

Again, these sets of tensions (they are not, of course, merely oppositions) form the axes along which, in the following chapters, I attempt to trace a series of ideas; axes which in turn twist, enlace, and cut across, crossing not only one another but those very boundaries of thought which concern philosophy itself. This is an exploration of those entanglements and transgressions, of the multiple crossings of boundaries.

Nietzschean temporality and the thought of eternal recurrence

> The centrifugal forces never flee the center for ever, but approach it anew only in order to retreat from it yet again.
> —Pierre Klossowski

Nietzsche warns us against the temptation to conflate metaphysics and grammar—to assume, that is, that the structure of Reality must correspond to that of the language in which we speak of it.[14] Nietzsche's concern is particularly with nouns, the words we use to name *things*, and their tendency to reify what they name. We cannot speak or write a language composed entirely of verbs and modifiers, and so we assume that there *are* things, identifiable extants with some stability over time. Here language gives us diachronic stability of identity. Things named are not eternal—beyond time—but at most sempiternal,[15] steady throughout time, the same each time they are named. In using language to name things, we implicitly deny the Hericlitean insight that "all is flux." The poet Paul Celan hints at the implicit lack of vitality in this fixity: "A word—you know/ a corpse."[16]

There is, of course, a limit to the timeliness of language, and that is precisely the limit that Nietzsche noted: to use words we must presume a stability in their meaning, yet time—whatever else it may be—is caught up, somehow, in transience (hence in instability). Words, after all, follow one another. Temporality is no more removable from language than is nomination, and so we find in our languages both the temporal and the sempiternal, while eternity, as Jabès suggests, remains silent: "Every birth breaks an original silence which it will fight to the death. Hence eternity is perhaps this mute, infinite time. . . ."[17] Eternity is missing from time as silence is from language—that is to say, as I shall argue in later chapters, it ruptures time at every instant, yet is a peculiar and particular absence of time. The very meaning of language, that element to which we are most inclined to grant eternity or at least sempiternity, can be gathered only across time, and not merely in a single direction, as we shall see. Thus it does not hold still at all, and may embody flux far better than we intend.

Nietzsche's most famous contribution to the thought of temporality is no doubt the deeply puzzling idea of the eternal return. This strange notion is vividly expressed in a passage from *The Gay Science:*

> What, if some day or night a demon were to steal after you into your loneliest loneliness and say to you: "This life as you now live it and have lived it, you will have to live once more and innumerable times more; and there will be nothing new in it, but every pain and every joy and every thought and sigh and everything unutterably small or great in your life will have to return to you, all in the same succession and sequence. . . ."
>
> Would you not throw yourself down and gnash your teeth and curse the demon who spoke thus? Or have you once experienced a tremendous moment when you would have answered him: "You are a god and never have I heard anything more divine."[18]

A literal interpretation of this idea would seem to have Nietzsche taking it rather directly from Arthur Schopenhauer, who pointed out that limited and conserved matter must, over infinitely extended time, form again into the patterns and sequences it has once known. In a sense, one could argue that time here remains metaphysically linear, yet the universe and its events circle over and over again, as if they constituted a wheel rolling along a sempiternal pathway. For Schopenhauer, however, the circle is truer than the line;[19] temporality, he argues, is a construct of human consciousness and nothing more.[20]

Nietzsche himself seems to have intended something rather different, given the intensity of his response to his own thought of recurrence, but it is difficult to be entirely certain. Michel Haar points out that the key words of the Nietzschean vocabulary, including *eternal return*, "elude conceptual logic" and "bring forth a plurality of meanings undermining any logic based on the principle of identity."[21] That is, appropriately enough, we can never quite pin these words down. What is more certain is that a number of twentieth-century thinkers, particularly among the literarily inclined French theorists, have understood the eternal return in ways which alter remarkably our understanding of time.

For Pierre Klossowski (whose work is influential on most later French thinkers who deal with Nietzsche), recurrence is not the deterministic repetition of the identical, but a rupture of the very possibility of identity, a demand for forgetfulness and for the affirmation of all possibilities of oneself as other than oneself.

> *Anamnesis* coincides with the revelation of the Return: how could the return not bring back forgetfulness? Not only do I learn that I (Nietzsche) have been brought back to the crucial moment in which the eternity of the circle culminates, the moment in which the truth of its necessary return is revealed to me; but at the same time I learn that I was *other* than I am *now* for having forgotten this truth, and thus that I have become another by learning it. Will I change again, and once more forget that I necessarily change during an eternity—until I relearn this revelation anew?[22]

The return demands this affirmation of loss because every possible variant will recur in the temporally-indefinite shuffling of matter. It demands that we affirm forgetfulness, because each thought of the eternal return will come to us as new, meaning—because it is itself recurrence—as already forgotten. Thus this cycle, which we might more readily see as a movement that guarantees, if not persistence, at least predictable sameness of movement and thus a sense of preservation, becomes for him a becoming caught up in utter loss. Curiously, the line along which recurrence rolls, under the tension of forgetting and loss, doubles back upon and cuts through itself. To see how this happens and to ask how we say it is in some ways the effort of all that follows here.

As I shall argue, loss becomes what is, almost, kept. (Blanchot writes, ". . . the law of the return, counting for all of the past and all of the future, will never allow you, except through a misunderstanding, to leave yourself a place in a possible present, nor to let any presence come as far as you."[23]) Later Gilles Deleuze will found his own work on the thought of a repetition inseparable from difference. In such repetition nothing is ever the same, where there are no originals but only an infinity of repeated instances, always, by the very act of repetition, different. Indeed, instances are repeatable only *because* of the differences, often including the difference in time, between them. For Deleuze as for Klossowski, repetition does not guarantee identity but breaks it. This is a most un-Schopenhauerian conception: "If you could ever nonetheless not be," suggests Schopenhauer in a rare moment of reassurance, "you would not be now."[24] "If you are now," these thinkers might respond, "nonetheless, you also are not."

Two other figures in this same tradition, because of their greater concern with language, will receive a more detailed consideration here. First is Maurice Blanchot, whose thought of time and silence forms not only my first chapter but also the heart of my own thought on these entangled subjects. Blanchot picks up on Klossowski's ideas, as well as those of many other traditions, to meditate upon the temporalities of silence in the fragmentation of language. For him, "The figure of return functions . . . as a paradoxical, but fatal and fateful exigency, one that reveals in the inevitability of death the impossibility of dying, in the law of repetition the excess of difference, in reason madness, and in the temptation to conclude, the necessity of infinite incompletion."[25] The second is Georges Bataille, his own language famously fragmented, who will emphasize the affirmation and intensity demanded by recurrence.

Even when we realize that Nietzsche diverges markedly from Schopenhauer (at least on certain readings), it is extraordinarily difficult genuinely to remove the thought of the eternal return from temporal linearity: this happens, we think, and *then* that happens, and *then* this happens *again*, and *before* it happens it had happened uncountably many times already. There is still a line here, a line in consciousness along which the circle rolls. We remain within Kantian subjectivity, the relentless temporality of experience. Instead, to think silence, we must think outside time (again with Blanchot, whom Michel Foucault rightly calls a thinker of the outside)—think this return as a tear in time.

eternity in time

> But to apprehend
> The point of intersection of the timeless
> With time, is an occupation for the saint—
> No occupation either, but something given
> And taken, in a lifetime's death in love
> —T. S. Eliot

We habitually assume that language measures for us the time of chronology, the time that lays out its length to be measured and does not double up, tear apart, fragment, and return in the process. Eternity, as return and rupture at once, is not a distention of time to immeasurability but is rather its outside. It is the immeasure, as Augustine will indirectly suggest, of silence.

It will take all this book even to begin a proper answer to the questions posed by the very thought of eternity—more precisely, to indicate the places of the questions themselves. Here only a few generalizations are possible. Eternity is not the same as time, not even an inconceivably long time, yet Peter Manchester rightly remarks in "The Religious Experience of Time and Eternity" that "Time and eternity make one topic, not two."[26] There he argues that "Eternity is something *intensive* about time rather than *extensive*, and it intensifies *something about time:* time as the bearer of ordering power, time as the figure of a living presence."[27] Taking up this statement in the context of the Bataillean thought that intensification may break, fragment, even seemingly invert the intensified (of this more in chapter two), we will be able to see as well eternity as the rupture of orders, the abandon of presence. Eternity as intensified time must be an absence and loss as well.

Traditionally, eternity is not infinite duration of time, but a "now" outside time. Even within this tradition, as I shall note in discussing Augustine, we find "now" to be such a slippery concept that both time and eternity become still more elusive than we would have thought. It is something intensive, an intensity of time so great that time shatters. Eternity does not return later along the line of time, always there in the same place; it cuts across the line. It is, I suspect, to use the spatial metaphors often helpful in thinking temporality, the vertical cut across the horizontal extension of time. Rainer Maria Rilke writes of ". . . speech where speaking/ Ends. Time/ standing perpendicular in the path of vanishing hearts."[28] Eternity, the following readings will suggest, stands perpendicular across the path of time (and in cutting through the continuity of the line, it problematizes the direction of time's path). It cuts through time as silence does through words, and indeed the cut of eternity is always a moment of silence.

We can sense already, or at least begin to sense, why the thought of eternity also demands that we think the emergence of silence within language, at the "fissure in time"[29] to which speaking and writing and reading can lead us, a silence that slices through time, an eternity that opens in the middle of the words enwrapping it. Within each mode of temporality, we can trace the murmur of silence; within the transgressive modes of the atemporal, we can indicate the shatter of words.

the silence of Heidegger

> It is not for me here to examine further the work of Heidegger,
> which has exerted such fascination—a term that already calls into
> question a way of thinking subject to a language which the play of
> etymology perhaps leads outside the field of philosophy, and
> which only ever affirms subject to the artful reservations of a nec-
> essarily disguised denegation.
>
> —Maurice Blanchot

One cannot, of course, undertake a discussion of silence in philosophy without some acknowledgement of the Heideggerian influence (particularly on
Blanchot, for whom the Heideggerian thoughts of "waiting" and "calling"
become central). Many of Heidegger's most central concerns are also my own:
memory in language, language as a call and as re-calling, the drawing of desire
across the space of an absence (of words across a space of silence). Heidegger
even contemplates the God who withdraws, a concept that will be of crucial
importance here: "How can man at the present stage of world history ask at
all seriously and rigorously whether the god nears or withdraws. . . ."[30] Real
differences, however, set the lines of thought I would explore here aside from
the path of Heidegger's (and of Nietzsche's, though the latter's insistence that
divergence is the most sincere form of discipleship makes any relation to his
work a bit more strange).

Heidegger, as Emmanuel Levinas points out, reverts always to the "truth
of Being," even in language. "Language . . . is the house of the truth of
Being,"[31] Heidegger writes, and it is "in its home [that] man dwells."[32] We
must not neglect the complexity of Heidegger's understanding, in which
Being is both near and far,[33] both turned away from us and that which somehow draws and addresses us.[34] Yet what draws us, he says, must "incline
toward us, toward our essential being, by appealing to our essential being as
what holds us there. To hold genuinely means to heed protectively. . . . What
keeps us in our essential being holds us only so long, however, as we for our
part keep holding on to what holds us. And we keep holding on to it by not
letting it out of our memory."[35] Truth, similar in its subtlety, is not for him
simple factuality, but an unveiling of a genuine essence and a "letting be" of
that essence.[36]

But it is precisely this unwavering devotion to an essence of truth, to an
unveilable (even if currently hidden) and full presence, to Being—the conviction that there is a revealing of the concealed, an arrival of the near, a
presence of the approaching, an unforgetful holding-in-memory, a home, a

dwelling, a truth—that the thinking of silence together with eternity finally cannot share. However devoutly we might wish that our memories held securely to that which held us too, we necessarily forget. The inadequacy of mortal memory is perhaps a Heideggerian version of original sin. In this sense that forgetfulness removes us from a full and reassuring presence, we move a bit closer to the Neoplatonism inherent in much apophatic theology. (This too will be more apparent later on, especially in chapters five and six.) *As us*, as "man" in Heidegger's terms, or as human more generally, we cannot hold on to memory. And when we do reach toward that which we cannot hold, that puzzling ultimate "memory," what "we" find is the loss of ourselves.

Overtly, Heidegger is antimetaphysical, primarily, it seems, in his insistence that Being is not a being, but pure giving-of-being, the truth of all that exists. "Metaphysics," he writes, "does not ask about the truth of Being itself. Nor does it therefore ask in what way the essence of man belongs to the truth of Being."[37] Yet despite his sense of openness, his insistence upon the importance of being silent in order to listen, Heidegger has too great a faith in stability, in beings participant in Being, who answer to their names.[38] Where my reading would differ from Heidegger's, then, is in denying that upon which he insists: a pure giving that is not the same as an abandonment, a pure truth that is not the absence but rather the fulfillment of all meaning, a dwelling which is home without exile.

Silence, eternity, and the thought of exile imply not a firm hold, even in memory, but a constant elusiveness, as much seductive as frustrating. Under the Nietzschean influence with the Klossowskian spin of forgetfulness, Heidegger's clear sense of origin and primacy too must slip out of place, even as his concerns retain their centrality.

the absent god

> God, so we read, is
> A part and a second, a scattered one:
> In the death of all those mown down
> He grows himself whole.
> —Paul Celan

As I have remarked, the concern with time as one topic together with eternity, and with language as one topic together with silence, becomes almost unavoidably (though never exclusively) a religious, especially a Judeo-Christian, concern. Judaism is a religion of the book and of textual exegesis elsewhere unmatched; Christianity is a religion founded in the sense of God as both body and word. As we shall see by the last chapter, the conception of divinity that emerges from the meditation on the axes time/ eternity, language/ silence is not quite standard in either tradition. It has, however, clear and important antecedents.

Within Jewish mysticism is a line of Kabbalistic thought that has proven unexpectedly appealing to some thinkers more generally Christian in background and concern (though not recognizably Christian in dogma), thinkers such as Blanchot, and again, though less directly, Bataille. It is also of considerable, somewhat less surprising, importance for another thinker whose work I shall take up here, Edmond Jabès, an Egyptian Jewish poet writing in French. This is the thought of Isaac Luria, a sixteenth-century mystic whose rather difficult work (known to us primarily through his students) postulates a God who creates the world by withdrawal, "the *deus absconditus*, the 'God who is hidden in his own self' and whose absence implies an absence from the world"—exile on a cosmic scale.[39] David Biale, in his discussion of Luria in *Jewish Mysticism in the Sixteenth Century*, notes that the *Tree of Life*, attributed to Luria, begins:

> Know that before all the emanations were emanated and the creations were created, the simple supernal light filled all existence and there was no empty space in the sense of vacant air or void, but everything was filled by this undifferentiated light. [This light] had neither beginning nor end . . . but was rather undifferentiated light that was entirely homogeneous and it was called the infinite light.
>
> And when it arose in his undifferentiated will to create the worlds. . . . He contracted Himself at the center-most point that was within Him and the light was contracted and withdrew towards the sides surrounding the central point, thus leaving an empty space, a vacuum, an empty void (where) the central point had been.[40]

Biale points out that "Luria . . . provided a theological and mystical dimension to the powerful feelings of exile experienced by so many Jews of the sixteenth century."[41] In a later stage of creation, after God's retreat makes possible the space of the world, the excessive strength of divine light overflows the restricted "vessels" into which God has intended its placement in his return from exile. After this, as Gershom Scholem writes, "nothing is perfect. . . . There is nothing that was not damaged by the breaking [of the vessels]. Nothing is in the place appointed for it. . . ."[42]

At first this may not sound very unusual. After all, absent or remote gods are not rare in the histories of religion. Mircea Eliade writes in *The Sacred and the Profane* that withdrawal is common to gods of the sky:

> Celestially structured supreme beings tend to disappear from the practice of religion, from cult: they depart . . . and become remote, inactive gods (*dei otiosi*). In short, it may be said of these gods that, after creating the cosmos, life, and man, they feel a sort of fatigue, as if the immense enterprise of the Creation had exhausted their resources. So they withdraw to the sky, leaving a son or a demiurge on earth to finish or perfect the Creation.[43]

Certain, especially Gnostic, traditions in the history of Christian thought have also posited a withdrawn God and the existence of a creative demiurge, but there the demiurge is the sole creator-god, and creation is not, especially in its material aspects, at all a good thing. (The parallels, however, are still strong; Scholem in fact "sees in the Jewish appropriation of Gnosticism the most vital element in the Kabbalah.")[44] In such traditions the true God can be found only by utter rejection of and separation from this world. A god whose withdrawal is itself truly creative seems to be absent from Christianity, yet is curiously consistent with some of the themes emergent from the lines of Christian thought I shall take up in later chapters.

Such a notion of positive withdrawal opens fascinating possibilities indeed; it is the opening of possibility itself. Although even Lurianic mysticism has in common with most mystical thought an emphasis on a re-attained oneness, it is not this unity but the creativity of withdrawal that strikes Blanchot, and along with him, most obviously, Jabès. Theirs is thought drawn to the sense of exile, of abandonment, more than to the process of reparation which would restore the world to its primordial wholeness (after which it would not, one presumes, be recognizably the world any longer). Divine withdrawal in Lurianic Kabbalism is not quite so grim as that of Manicheaism, in which the withdrawal of God means the privation of good, so that the world left behind is (at least insofar as it is material, a sense it shares with gnosticism generally) purely evil—though there too there is a sense that while God has taken most of the light with him, some may be refindable. Practice based on this Kabbalistic tradition, in fact, entails prayerful meditation by which the "divine sparks" absent from the dark world are to be restored with human help.[45] Indeed, light must be refindable, unless we are to be without hope altogether. Religious advocacy of pure despair has been rare.

Ultimately, I would propose a reading of withdrawal which differs significantly from Luria's in lacking the optimistic anticipation of rejoining, yet is in itself more positive—a reading which seems to me to be more nearly in line with Blanchot and emergent, as we shall see, in the thought of numerous others. Biale points out that Lurianic Kabbalah gives various answers to the question of the reason for God's contraction; that which I have found most intriguing, if paradoxical, is the first: "One is that God willed the contraction in order to create the world as a result of his overflowing love."[46] Although Biale sees as "much more radical" a second answer, that God was endeavoring to rid himself of disharmonious elements,[47] I hope to trace out some rather radical and surprising implications of the first—of this overflow and contraction somehow mysteriously identical. Here, of course, are still stronger traces of Neoplatonism, but with a far greater emphasis on exile.

Specifically, if we take seriously the idea that time and eternity make one subject, and that silence and language make one subject, then perhaps too this abandon and exile make one subject with the peculiar concern of redemption. God's withdrawal, says Jabès, opens the space for the word. God's silence makes possible our speaking. The generous withdrawal of abandonment makes possible our very being, even our being-in-exile, in the inadequacies of the human word. Perhaps, these intersections suggest, exile and redemption are not *only* one subject, but are one subject too. God, says Luria, created not only everything but also nothing: "God creates nothingness out of himself by contracting himself (zimzum). Every act of creation requires a space devoid of God. . . ."[48] So, we might say, everything and nothing are co-created, and in the beginning God says, and in silence withdraws the saying.

Silence cuts across a great many of the modes or "uses" (the technological implication is suspect) of language. Thus in my explorations here I have drawn on work and thought across several verbal disciplines. I cannot do full justice to any of these thinkers—each merits the several volumes devoted to his work—and I recognize that the angle of approach through time and silence often makes for an odd perspective. It has seemed to me, as Leslie Hill remarks of Blanchot's work in *The Infinite Conversation*, "that, in order to respond faithfully to a text, it is necessary to respond, not to those elements in a text—concepts or arguments, topics or themes—which are easily repeated, and which, once repeated, in fact betray the text, but rather to that in the text—a tone, a slippage, an accident, or an incoherence—which cannot be named as such and thus seemingly resists repetition."[49] In each of the texts to which I have endeavored to respond, the complex and multiple intersection time/silence/eternity/language slips, in various ways.

Some of these thinkers are recognized, at least in some traditions, as philosophers. As I have mentioned, in conceiving the peculiar self-redeeming character of language in time, I have begun with an effort to work through some of the temporalities of silence in the thought of Maurice Blanchot. My approach here, as in the subsequent discussion, has been less exegetical or even analytical than interactive: I have attempted to think these temporalities with the help of, and under the influence of, Blanchot's work. Following this I have take up Georges Bataille's concern, deriving from, but by no means fully continuous with, the mystical tradition of ineffability, with language shattered by intensity (a central concern of Bataille's), and with the peculiar effects of intensity upon human time. From this I move into a discussion of the language of poetry—not all poetry, of course, but the work of four poets for whom the concerns of time, silence, exile, and their seeming opposites are central: Jabès, Hölderlin, Celan, and Rilke.

I turn then to a more overt version of the theological concerns that have already appeared in the discussion, beginning with a look at Augustine's frustrated yet illuminating take on time and memory in the *Confessions*, continuing with some of the sermons of Meister Eckhart, whose take on mysticism, some half a millennium prior to Bataille's, was every bit as strange.

And some insight from each of these thinkers who follow will be illuminating for all the others, betraying in their repetition the slippage of thought into silence. The framing of the question itself must be Blanchot's, and his insights into silence as absent, unkeepable, and yet inherent in language have informed all of my other readings. From Bataille in particular I take the importance of a sense of temporal intensification in its effects upon language as fragmenting and upon memory as an unsatisfiable demand. The poetic works will give us a sense of the reach toward an impossible original word, of exile from that origin, of time extended opposed to time attended-to. St. Augustine offers a sense of language as so intimate to time that we can scarcely think them apart afterwards, and a single haunting phrase: "I am certain that I remember forgetfulness itself." Meister Eckhart gives to the absence of origin an important and surprising double sense of joy and necessary forgetfulness. Finally, in conclusion, we return to the overarching questions, to find time and eternity in language and silence, to find the cut across which cannot be kept. We return to the beginning, and in the beginning, we know, is the word.

chapter one

*I*mmemorial silence: Maurice Blanchot

beginning to speak

Blanchot shows that all commentary is necessarily unfaithful. It's
one of the things that distinguishes him from Heidegger.
—Leslie Hill

Writing of a writer like Maurice Blanchot, notable for his gracefully elliptical economy of expression, is virtually guaranteed to make one's own prose
clumsy and inept. I must confess that I feel in trying to write of Blanchot
what he may have felt in writing, in 1990, "I shall begin to write again, not
on Derrida, (how pretentious!) but with his help, and convinced that I shall
betray him immediately."[1] This inept betrayal may be particularly apparent
here, since the issues I would engage are, Blanchot says, found in "neither
reading nor writing, nor speaking. . . ."[2] Here I shall address the questions of
time and silence by writing both with and about his work, about a particularly seductive and disturbing cluster of issues in his work, aware that
addressing directly the elliptical openness of these texts risks chattering over
their silences.

To write with the help of—or, more honestly, under the influence of—
other thinkers is to write with those whose work opens spaces of possibility
for one's own thought, and few can do this so astonishingly well as Blanchot.
In fact, it is precisely this ability of Blanchot's to open spaces that is so surprising in his work, and so disturbing, which is why before writing further of
Blanchot it may be advisable to say something of reading him. I began my
own reading of Blanchot under the influence of others (chiefly Bataille and

17

Foucault) with the collections of literary essays, eventually making my way to one of his "fragmentary" (or, more properly, unclassifiable) works, *The Step Not Beyond*.[3] In this text passages ranging in length from sentence fragments to a few pages are set apart from one another, each given space to resonate, each opening up space around itself. This formula is followed as well in *The Writing of the Disaster* and *The Infinite Conversation*, and it is on this trio that I shall focus here. The thought to which these texts expose us is as unfamiliar as Blanchot says, in the second sentence of *The Step Not Beyond*, death is—the sentence reads in English, "To death we are not accustomed."[4] And I found, after reading that sentence, that I had to put the book down for several hours, simply to make room for what was indeed unaccustomed thought.

More exactly, Blanchot opens spaces in language, in reading, and in thinking that are terrifying for being at once of the nature of things we should have known, or are sure that we once knew, and utterly unfamiliar. These are the spaces that were always just outside what we know, spaces before which we find ourselves utterly insecure. And because it is where we are most insecure and the matters before us are most unfamiliar that thinking is at its most exciting, I have decided, whether perversely or just foolishly, to try to explore, just a little bit, those very spaces, those openings in the intertwinings of language and time. In the space of the unfamiliar and already known, we find the memory of a shattered present, an immemorial silence. I have tried to write here of what was and is every time again so astonishing to read: of silence and its remarkable temporality.

One senses in Blanchot a longing for silence ("Silence is impossible. That is why we desire it."[5]) which cannot be kept and will not allow itself to be said, which eludes us and yet places on us the demands of language itself. It is silence that gives to Blanchot's work its paradoxical rigor, a silence that is at once the space into which he writes (that which calls for his writing; that which calls to his thinking) and that which he cannot preserve in his writing. Cannot, because silence, as he tells us, cannot be kept; because writing shares with speaking the attribute of breaking the very silence that calls to it. Silence calls to language, and to keep silent would no more preserve silence than would speaking or writing of it. The call of silence reverberates, in a muffled way, within language itself.[6]

One ground of the unkeepability of silence is in fact its curious relation to the temporal. In Blanchot's work the slipping and shifting of time will link silence to both madness and death, to time gone mad in the thought of eternal recurrence and to time gone missing in an unthinkable absence. I would suggest, too, that we find here the slightest edge of joy: "Perhaps," as Blanchot suggests, "we know the disaster by other, perhaps joyful names. . . ."[7]

Yet this madness is disaster still. Silence in Blanchot is a gentle violence, a quiet devastation. It works its violence by fragmentation, a fragmentation not only of language but also of time, caught up for us in language—not only in its tenses, but in the passage of our speaking and writing and reading, in the effort to gather up meaning across the passage of a sentence, in our wait for the time at the end of the sentence in which we shall expect to remember its meaning. The fear which silence evokes, the ancient fear, is the fear of time and the absence of time, time which is never more than the coming of an absence, time which is not gathered into memory but fragmented in the return. But this silence, this absence, is also an opening. The infinite spaces which terrify are still the joyous openings which invite.

We can see in Blanchot's use of silence a temporality of past, present, and future. In his thought, under the Nietzschean influence, silence is implicated in the eternal recurrence. I have found that it is easiest to speak of silence first in its future aspect, as the call; then in its present aspect, as that which empties presence; then in its past aspect, as that which we find ourselves unable to remember or forget—from which we shall see that it has returned, before and after, already. Or, more precisely, we find that the temporality of silence is that of forgetting and returning, a temporal evocation of absence within every mode of time.

the opening onto the future:
silence as invitation and waiting

You were my death:
you I could hold
when all fell away from me.
—Paul Celan

At one level anticipatory or future-oriented silence is fairly straightforward, though it opens immediately onto complexity. Silence makes conversation possible. Simply, there must be silence to call forth speaking, or even writing. Silence is in this sense an invitation into a future, a space that draws us forth. Often we fail to find or make such silence: we speak over and across one another, interrupt, drown out, ignore one another. But aside from the fact that few of us consider such discursive situations ideal, we realize that such speaking-over fails to be a response; it is ir-responsible; it is, we might even say, uncalled-for. To speak over, to write without regard for the space into which one writes, to think while keeping one's mind closed to the outside, is to evade the infinite conversation invited by the pause, the opening, the silence that waits before us. It is to speak as if one owned language, rather than being dispossessed by it, by its refusal of any possession.[8]

Simply, ideally, we are called by such silence, which is neither awkward nor angry. The easy, gracious silence is what Blanchot calls "the legitimate pause, the one permitting the give and take of conversation, the benevolent, intelligent pause" or "that beautifully poised waiting with which two inter-locutors, from one shore to another, measure their right to communicate."[9] Such silence draws forth response; it is conversational. In fact, we begin to speak only by anticipating this silence—we speak, that is, toward the possi-bility of response. "Every beginning speech begins by responding; a response to what is not yet heard, an attentive response in which impatient waiting for the unknown and the desiring hope for presence are affirmed."[10] We speak, then, not only in order to be heard but to open up the space in which we might hear something new. From outside ourselves, new words enter and open new questions in turn.

Neither the wait nor the pause, though, is ever simple or wholly legiti-mate. In speaking toward the possibility of response, even in writing to be read, we await an interruption or disruption. More precisely, we open a space of interrogation. All speech is questioning in its anticipation of response; every response is another question. The conversation is infinite; there is always another opening. "As soon as there is a question, there is no reply that could exhaust that question,"[11] Blanchot writes, a sentiment that Jabès (whose work Blanchot admires) will extend to the infinite question that humanity, for him, poses to God. And interrogation is the mode of speech proper not only to the future which we await but to that which we try, in awaiting, to avoid; or that for which we await an end, thinking that then it can never come again: that is, to madness.[12] "Strictly," Blanchot writes of madness, "we maintain this word in the interrogative position: Hölderlin was mad, but was he?" and then: "Madness would thus be a word in perpetual incongruance with itself and interrogative throughout, such that it would put into question its possibility and, through it, the possibility of language that would admit it, thus would put interrogation itself into question. . . ."[13]

Silence is as proper to madness, which interrogates language, for Blan-chot as for Foucault, who saw in madness the silence imposed by the discourse of rationality.[14] Blanchot writes, ". . . what is being constituted in silence—in the seclusion of the Great Confinement, and through a movement that answers to the banishment pronounced by Descartes—is the very world of Unreason," inclusive not only of madness but as well of "sexual prohibitions,

religious interdicts, and all the excesses of thought and heart."[15] The pause
constituted by silence is a break, and in it language is indeed broken; in the
silence of madness it is cut open, put into question: "madness reveals a stag-
gering depth, a subterranean violence, a knowledge that is boundless, devas-
tating, and secret."[16]

Blanchot himself distinguishes this devastation that drives language
mad from the more gentle conversational pause, although we know that gentleness will open onto the extreme. "I will say rather: nothing extreme
except through gentleness,"[17] he writes, reminding us of the impossible quiet
passivity of the wait which, as we shall see, interrogates speaking. Even this
gentle responsivity participates in madness. "We have," he tells us, "two
important distinctions . . . the pause that permits exchange, the wait that
measures infinite distance. But in waiting it is not simply the delicate rupture preparing the poetic act that declares itself, but also, and at the same
time, other forms of arrest that are very profound, very perverse, more and
more perverse, and always such that if one distinguishes them, the distinction does not avert but rather postulates ambiguity."[18] In gentleness we find
one of the central ambiguities of silence; this gentleness (this passive wait
before the future) is itself an extreme, a devastation or disaster murmuring
to us of the inherent violence of the most quiet, which is silence, and the
most passive, which is waiting.[19]

What is it we await? What throws all of our meaning into question,
interrogates us endlessly, draws us to an impossibility? In the context of infinite interrogation, this question is itself illegitimate. What is it we await,
which cannot arrive, at which we cannot arrive even at the end of our waiting?[20] A simple answer is a lie which still comes close to a truth: in the future,
throwing everything into question; in silence, working within language, is
death. "Death, this badly unified word, interrogation always displaced." [21]
Death, like madness, can be posed only in the interrogative.

The answer claiming that what we await is death is a lie because it names,
with the definition and identifiability that naming implies, as if we had
answered the question. Death is not what we await, any more than madness is
the question we ask. Yet it is linked to a pure waiting as madness is linked to
pure interrogation. "'Death' is not capable of putting an end to waiting,"[22]
Blanchot says; the wait is infinite, the awaited the impossible. We wait and we
invite; we play our sense of the future between action and passivity. We invite
a doubly impossible silence: the infinite awaiting, always an opening and invitation, the call which reverberates in language without language being able to
speak it; and the unawaitable, the impossible necessity of death,[23] the silent
violence of destruction, the madness at the heart of meaning.

Every invitation, that is, is at once creative and destructive: "'Enter into the destructive element,' we do not write a word that does not contain this invitation and sometimes, another that is superfluous: let you destroy yourself."[24] The destructive invitation (the silent opening allied with madness and death) is forgetfulness: "To speak is to lose rather than to retain; to entrust to forgetfulness rather than to memory. . . ."[25]

Against the forgetfulness of speaking, we think, we have writing. But here, too, we are invited to silence, not just by mad writing (such as Hölderlin's, which, as we shall see in chapter three, warns us of our own inability to speak what is most profound) but by all writing, as the invitation to destruction. (This issue will recur in the discussion of Bataille's work as well.) Death and forgetting are entangled in writing as in speaking, though the relation is no longer so natural: ". . . writing is always second in the sense that, even if nothing precedes it, it does not pose as first, instead ruining all primacy through an indefinite reference that leaves no place even for the void. Such is, then, barely indicated, the dispersed violence of writing, a violence by which speech is always already set apart, effaced in advance and no longer restored, violence, it is true, that is not natural and that also prevents us, dying, from dying a natural death."[26] Writing is violence enacted on language. To write is already to open, to cut apart language for the spaces of silence: ". . . there is no silence if not written: broken reserve, a deep cut in the possibility of any cut at all."[27] "The game of common etymology makes of writing a cutting movement, a tear, a crisis . . . the proper tool for writing was also proper to incising: the stylet . . . this incisive reminder still invokes a cutting operation, if not a butchery: a kind of violence. . . ."[28] In writing we find dying, the impossibility of death, as the infinite wait for that which will put no end to waiting; in speaking we find madness in an endless interrogation. Yet writing also enters into the interrogation of the infinite conversation as it directs itself toward the reader; speaking, naturally (too naturally, Blanchot says) evokes death in the silence of the voice.

Silence is waiting in language. It waits for and as the answer to an unposable question, as time gone missing and mad; yet it remains itself an interval of interrogation, awaiting what will come from outside. It opens in language the spaces in which we will forget, a forgetfulness we anticipate with hope (that we can forget madness and render it truly impossible; that we will receive to our question an answer at last) and with fear (that we shall forget meaning, and madness will fill its space; that death awaits as the final lack of an answer).

And so we are invited to the destruction of meaning. We are invited, at the beginning of speaking, to forget: "to speak is to draw from the depths of speech an inexhaustible forgetfulness."[29] We wait, "waiting for nothing," only, always again, "opening the interval of another waiting."[30] "To death we are not accustomed," nor can we become so. But our desire here is not simply to retreat: "the preoccupation with dying, throughout Blanchot's work, is less in the service of negativity or nihilism than of radical passion, irreducible extremity, and boundless affirmation."[31] Here the passivity of the wait is affirmed as surely and as paradoxically as the ineluctable and infinite return is for Nietzsche.

Silence, then, is a mode of waiting, of hope and fear, the opening of the future which may be the madness of the return and the unthinkable of death. In opening language to the not-yet of the future, silence must also alter the relation of language and thought to presence, with which it is in constant battle.[32] And so we slide, already through the detour of forgetting, to another temporality in our search for a present reality.

present language: silence as disruption and secret

> If, from the start, a mind regarded the boundary between reason and unreason . . . as a flagrant error, it would consent to reason only if it could also reserve for itself the use of unreason.
> —Pierre Klossowski

Present in language, we say, or more precisely that which language presents, is meaning. Silence, too, is present, or not-present, concealed and revealed, lacking a name. Which is to say that silence is the absence of and in language, the break in meaning. As absence, too, silence is linked to madness: "That madness is present in every language is not enough to establish that it is not omitted in them."[33] Absent from every language is what would turn madness to reason.[34] Silence is antithetical to the presence of meaning, but never purely so, because meaning is still in need of silence: "A word that is almost deprived of meaning is noisy. Meaning is limited silence (language is relatively silent, depending on the degree to which it contains the element into which it departs, the already departed, the absent meaning, which verges upon the a-semic)."[35] Pure noise means nothing.

Both speaking and writing, as we have already begun to see in the effort to understand waiting within them, lose presence. Speech, awaiting the silence that is its future yet interrogates it throughout, slides immediately into the past: ". . . speech is perishable. Scarcely said, it is effaced, lost without recourse. It forgets itself."[36] Writing, directed in hope to a future reader, can never be read (properly speaking) by its writer, and loses its hope of a future even as it fails to preserve a past, once more without presence, or in "obscure combat" with presence: "It is . . . in struggling for presence (in accepting to make itself naively the memorial of something that presents itself in it) that language treacherously destroys it. This happens by way of writing."[37]

It is Blanchot's work, the work of his unworking,[38] to foreground the silent presence of absence. What he would speak, and write, what he would think and say and present to us, is always a secret, necessarily so, a secret which cannot be kept, just as we cannot keep silence. Michael Newman remarks, "The secret can neither be told nor not told, and this is the paradox of testimony: as Blanchot writes. . . , 'The secret alluded to is that there is none, except for those who refuse to tell.—But it is unutterable inasmuch as narrated, proffered.' The very telling, in other words, obscures what is to be told."[39] One cannot, could not even if one could write as gracefully as Blanchot, tell and keep the secret. And yet the secret, that which is absent or unspeakable at the heart of meaning, reverberates throughout the work. Writing is not an act of presenting but a call, an invitation to share the secret which cannot be shared. It calls to the absence of meaning: "May what is written resound in the stillness, making silence resound at length, before returning to the motionless peace where the enigma still wakes."[40]

With this, absence takes on a familiar resonance. The secret we cannot share (the meaning that hollows out the center of every meaning, the madness at the heart of reason) is shared by all, is death: "It is the dying which, though unsharable, I have in common with all."[41] With Freud, Blanchot links death to silence as the inability to present meaning: "If it is true that for a certain Freud, 'our unconscious cannot conceive of our own mortality' (is unable to represent mortality to itself), then it would seem to follow that dying is unrepresentable, not only because it has no present, but also because it has no place, not even in time, the temporality of time."[42] For Freud, too, the violence of the death drive is silent; the destructive force is manifest—visible or audible—only when it is intermingled with the forces favoring life. And for Freud, too, the experience which breaks through experience, which so exceeds the possibility of experience as to enter straightaway into the atemporality of the unconscious, will call to us through and without language, in which it has, nonetheless, no place.

The call, once more, is to entry into destruction. Death, as the drive to destroy, is violence, and it calls silently from within language. "Violence is at work in language and, more decidedly, in the speech of writing, in as much as language conceals itself from work: this action of concealing itself again belongs to violence."[43] To make secret and to reveal belong alike to the violence of destruction. From Freud to Bataille to Deleuze to Blanchot we are reminded of something astonishing: violence is silent.[44] And silence, in all of its gentleness, is violent still.

Because violence is silent, because death is a shared and yet unspeakable secret, we know that we lie in naming it. We try to name it, to not-keep its secret, in order to lose it or rid ourselves of it; we try to forget it. ". . . we have lost death," Blanchot says. ". . . We name it, but in order to master it through a name and, through this name, finally rid ourselves of it."[45] But we cannot forget it. First, death itself forgets us; it is the arrival of our absence. Second, we have never known it; it was never there for us to forget, any more than it ever came at the end of our awaiting. We have never known what it was; it warns us of the impossibility of knowing. Finally, like madness, it keeps its own secret within the language that tries to name it.

We are faced with what we cannot face and cannot even present to ourselves, the muffled reverberations of madness and death within language, in silence. We must ask, too, what it is that renders the present impossible, keeps it from being a present now, even if it waits. The return, we might say, a return which is no comfort. Schopenhauer saw the eternal return as the *guarantor* of presence.[46] But for Blanchot, the return is a reminder of what we have always already forgotten, of the impossible un-knowledge that comes to us only by way of forgetting. "We must pass by way of this knowledge and forget it."[47] We must forget that we have passed already. "Know only," we are instructed, knowing that we cannot know, "—injunction that does not present itself—that the law of the return, counting for all of the past and all of the future, will never allow you, except through a misunderstanding, to leave yourself a place in a possible present, nor to let any presence come as far as you."[48] Further, we are warned, "The Eternal Return of the Same: the having been, repetition of a will take place as having been, does not signal any presence, even that of old. The Eternal Return would say this, it would say that in what has been, no present is retained, except in this speaking of it, if it were spoken."[49] And in this speaking, too, it is exactly the present which eludes us.

And so silence opens onto the future as the invitation to language, but also to (self-) destruction, to knowing the secret that cannot be known. It opens within the present to tell us—that is, to keep secret from us, though it can neither tell nor keep the secret—of the absence that opens up within the very meaning language endeavors to present. It tells us that it is death we await, though this name, "death," lies by naming. It tells us that madness is at the heart of all our meanings, though we lie by pretending to be able to say without question "madness." But where, if it is never present, do we find meaning, the meaning for which we wait? What limits the silence, if not only noise? Only one answer remains: we seek meaning in memory; it is only when speaking has passed or writing has been read that, we think, we know what we have waited to know: what it means. (As we shall later, somewhat surprisingly, see, this connection of meaning to memory-in-silence may be found in the reflections of Augustine as well.)

past silence: memory is the dispersal of fragmentation

> Sentences will be confined to museums if the emptiness of writing persists.
>
> —Georges Bataille

It seems that here, at least and at last, we might find some security: in that which we hold in memory. Memory, as Heidegger tells us, is the gathering of recollection,[50] where we might collect the bits of our knowledge and bring them back to coherence. But silence, once more, opens this secure space from within, fragments what memory has patiently collected, "linking us to a past without memory."[51] We feel that we shall come to meaning only in memory; "I do not know," Blanchot writes, "but I have the feeling that I'm going to have known."[52] In this feeling, though, memory is already caught up into the expectation of the future and implicated in the impossible necessity of the return.

Again, this is no simple return which would allow us to remember because what happens now mirrors what happened once; rather, it is a decentered return which means that whatever happens we have always, already, forgotten.

> [T]he infinite of the return . . . does not permit assigning to the figure a center, even less an infinity of centers, just as the infinite of the repetition cannot be totalized in order to produce the unity of a figure strictly delimited and whose construction would escape the law it figures forth. If the Eternal Return can affirm itself, it affirms neither the return as circle, nor the primacy of the One, nor the Whole, and not even by way of the necessity that through the Eternal Return 'everything returns,' . . . it is not the whole that returns, but rather: it returns, the return returns. [53]

Such a return does not join our moments into a single smooth circle but breaks them irrevocably apart, in the space where silence fragments and disjoins endlessly our efforts at meaning. In this fragmentation we find no gathering again, but "forgetfulness, remembrance of the immemorial, without recollection."[54]

Silence calls us to an unknown, to the outside/within of language. Yet our sense of this unknown is not pure future—that which we *shall* find—nor is it presence, as if we could see it before us. Silence calls to memory, to our sense of having forgotten. It calls, more precisely, to what we could never remember, never re-collect, because it began without origin, in fragmentation, as the very site of disruption. (This nonorigin, this break will recur in some form in the thought of everyone we read in this work.)

Forgetting, Blanchot says, (surprisingly at first) is thus older and deeper than memory. "Forgetting is the primordial divinity, the venerable ancestor and first presence of what, in a later generation, will give rise to Mnemosyne. . . . The essence of memory is therefore forgetting; the forgetfulness of which one must drink in order to die."[55] This is not a secondary forgetting, failing what we once knew or even remembered;[56] it is a primordial forgetting of what we never knew, but always knew, somehow, that we would have known. All is past, all has already passed not into the safe recollection of memory but into the silence of pure loss—"*had he then forgotten it, the meeting always to come that had, however, always already taken place, in an eternal past, eternally without present?*"[57]

Forgetting, already caught up in the return, can only come first because that which is to come has passed already. But it has passed away, as Blanchot argues writing does, without a trace, without leaving marks.[58] In silence we forget what we never remembered, what was always silent, just beyond our hearing. Forgetfulness partakes of the impossible passivity we have already seen in waiting: ". . . forgetting gets away. It escapes. This does not simply mean that through forgetting a certain possibility is taken from us and a certain impotence revealed, but rather that the possibility that is forgetting is a slipping outside of possibility."[59]

Memory is the gathering of recollection; forgetting is the silent dispersal of fragmentation.[60] What we forget; our "remembrance" of the immemorial, is that in which we have (impossibly) lost ourselves. "[I]mpossible loss," as Blanchot remarks in writing of Bataille, ". . . does not allow the tensions which rip thought apart, and which the harshness of a restless language maintains, to congeal into a system."[61] We will try to speak of the impossible, or to silence it; we will try to speak it in order to silence it. But silence will break forth impossibly from the places in which we try to keep it, returning to the outside we have forgotten. "Still, nothing is said," as we are warned, "if we do not force ourselves to think . . . the invisible rupture of prohibition, the transgression to which we feel we are accessories, because it is also our own strangeness."[62]

What we must force ourselves to think—the silence without which nothing is said—is our own transgression, the breaking of our own limits. We are, in this silent space, this space without origin into which we come only by returning, returning to the forgotten. This inexplicable-seeming movement, return by forgetting, will recur in a number of the readings that follow, building new senses in each elaboration. "[F]ragmentation is bound up with the revelation of the Eternal Return. The eternal return says time as an eternal repetition, and fragmentary speech repeats this repetition by stripping it of any eternity."[63] Eternity as the standing now would be an infinite presence; speech fragmented by silence bespeaks an infinite absence. We must return to the immemorial.

immemorial silence: thought from the outside

We are standing on the edge of an abyss that had long been invisible: the being of language only appears for itself with the disappearance of the subject.
                                                            —Michel Foucault

Primordial forgetting, which is also the forgetting without origin, implies the immemorial: it forgets what we did not originally remember. The immemorial implies the inexperiencable: we cannot remember what we could never know. Time is caught again in a return that makes it both necessary and meaningless. We cannot remember that which has never entered the possibility of memory. It is the moment of such impossibility, intensity, or intolerability—of pain or joy or both at once—the never-present instant of mortal intensity at the quick of life, which refuses the possibility of memory by refusing presence: "The quick of life would be the burn of a wound—a hurt so lively, a flame so avid that it is not content to live and be present, but consumes all that is present till presence is precisely what is exempt from the present. The quick of life is the exemplarity . . . of un-presence . . . absence in its vivacity always coming back without ever coming."[64]

Such moments are without original, because (as the reading of Bataille will make more apparent) *we* were never there: "There is no origin, if origin

presupposes an original presence. Always past, long since past already, something that has passed without being present—such is the immemorial which
gives us forgetfulness saying: every beginning is a beginning over."[65] It is only
in having-forgotten these unpresented moments that we come to them; we
come to them always as to something we have forgotten.

This is so first via Blanchot's embrace of the idea of eternal recurrence.
On his reading, as on Klossowski's, return demands that I forget. But we also
come to the already forgotten. As I shall argue in more detail in the next
chapter, moments of the greatest intensity may never make it to consciously
accessible memory. And that which we have primordially forgotten is, once
more, death: "Through the movement that steals away (forgetting), we allow
ourselves to turn toward what escapes (death), as though the only authentic
approach to this inauthentic event belonged to forgetting. Forgetting, death:
the unconditional detour."[66] We cannot move through time without detour,
even towards death. But, if we can succeed in the passivity which can be no
success of ours, we are able to forget, to open to the outside beyond experience. If we are able to allow it, we can read Blanchot, and have the feeling,
at the limit of madness, that we are going to have known silence. "It is . . . in
the space established between madness and unreason . . . that we have to ask
ourselves if it is true that literature and art might be able to entertain these
limit-experiences and thus, beyond culture, pave the way for a relation with
what culture rejects: a speech of borders, the outside of writing."[67]

Between the madness of the return (by way of the unconditional detour
outside of time) and the unreasoning absence of meaning, we come back—
yet we come for the first time—to those spaces from which we were always
absent, in which we had always lost ourselves. Back to the outside, which we
have forgotten. "To remember forgetfully: again, the outside."[68] Back to death
and to madness—and to joy beyond ourselves. Back to the spaces in which
the languages by which we constitute ourselves, our self-inscriptions and our
voices, fall, always have fallen, silent.

Silent and yet wanting, though lacking nothing. This is the joy of desire.
For there is desire in forgetfulness, as much as fear; there is desire for fear,
even, for life at its most intense and for the mortal excesses of madness;
"desire for that which provokes the fear that nothing provokes."[69] It is the
desire belonging to the outside, "the thought that thinks more than it
thinks."[70] Such a desire, we are told, "desires what the one who desires has no
need of, what is not lacking and what the one who desires has no desire to
attain, it being the very desire for what must remain inaccessible and for-
eign. . . ."[71] Only in forgetting do we open space for such desire, a "mute and
closed space where desire endlessly wanders."[72] This is a desire to exceed our

own limits, a desire that will take us beyond ourselves, such that the desire and its fulfillment, which in the end we shall be unable to distinguish from one another, are beyond our ability to say them. Indeed, we cannot know these joys which take us beyond the limits of knowing. This is, as Blanchot writes of Bataille's affirmation of the inexperiencable limit-experience, "an affirmation of which man has no memory . . . a measure of extreme pain and extreme joy."[73]

The extreme, the limit, the outside: this is the silent space which calls to us, draws us back before ourselves, in a repetition which the Deleuzean reading of Freud would tie in turn to the drive for death,[74] to a space that can only be one to which we return, never for the first time. It is to this return that silence, murmuring incessantly beneath Blanchot's words, calls us.

Here the return pulls me back to those astonishing and terrifying opening lines of *The Step Not Beyond*. We have already read the second line, "To death we are not accustomed." The first is an invitation. *Let us enter into this relation*,[75] Blanchot invites; the secret is shared among us; let us enter into what relates us, reverberates across us, and yet marks (with the mark that writing never leaves) the infinite distances between us. The mortal distances: To death we are not accustomed. A fragment set next to our relation and yet broken apart from it; a fragment that relates and fragments us, measures between us the infinite distance that constitutes our relation. We will have known, surely, but we shall not remember.

This is what the thought of the eternal return tells us: it is not our presence, but our passing, which is guaranteed. It is mortality which reverberates within this mad thought; it is at mortal intensity that Blanchot writes, "In the mortal intensity, the fleeing silence of the countless cry."[76] Death whispers silently, madly, in the voice of no one (the murmur of the neuter, the impersonal) throughout Blanchot's texts, as the return unworks his remarkably meticulous (his beautifully worked-out) writings. But mortality, loss of self, is not only the ancient fear; it is the within-outside, which is at the same time the space into which we leave ourselves at the height of joy: extreme joy, extreme pain. To destroy oneself, to accept the invitation into the destructive element, is not an act of hatred. We do not hate where we forget: "*Lethe* is also the companion of Eros, the awakening proper to sleep, the distance from which one cannot take one's distance since it comes in all that moves away. . . ."[77] This seductive distancing is an infinite demand: ". . . as though impossibility, that by which we are no longer able to be able, were waiting for us behind all that we live, think, and say—if only we have been once at the end of this waiting, without ever falling short of what this surplus or addition, this surplus of emptiness, of 'negativity,' demanded of us and that is in us the infinite heart of the passion of thought."[78] From this sense, which evolves in Blanchot's understanding of Bataille (for whom the return is caught up in the impossible nonknowledge of communication, which opens us to one another without making any union possible), we can turn to one of Bataille's own thoughts (with which I return to the thought that first brought me to Blanchot): "What is strangest is that nonknowledge should have the ability to sanction. As if, from the outside, it had been said to us: 'Here you are at last.'"[79]

Here we are, at last. Let us enter into this relation.

$\mathcal{A}$nd my memory from the minds of men: Georges Bataille

the rigor of fragmentation

> Driven into the
> terrain
> with the unmistakable track:
>
> grass, written asunder.
>> —Paul Celan

Much of contemporary French theory, and theory under that influence, adheres stubbornly to one of Nietzsche's convictions: that the will to systematicity is a lack of integrity. Many other theorists, of course, consider this adherence a willful defiance of theoretical discipline. If we deny the demand for systematic order and coherence, such thinking goes, then we can toss anything at all into our theoretical constructs, and even contradictions can be dismissed—we are postmodern, we contain multitudes. To those annoyed by such multiplicity, such defiance, Georges Bataille stands as a negative exemplar, a philosopher who might better have remained, as he also was, a pornographer, or resigned himself to the quiet obscurity of, as he also was, a medievalist librarian. To those drawn by such thought, on the other hand, Bataille is among the most intriguing of thinkers, in his multidisciplinarity as much as in his fragmentary, Nietzschean-influenced style.

In fragmentary sentences and hyperbolic paragraphs, Bataille writes of sensuality, religious feeling, drunkenness, and sleepless nights. His writing,

writing in order not to go mad, not infrequently seems its own form of madness.[1] But with the madness that it is not, this writing shares the paradoxical
rigor of silence in words. Bataille's is the rigor of intensification, in which
transgression is a matter not of ignoring the rules but of applying them so
severely that they work against themselves to the point of inversion. I would
argue that Bataille neither ignores nor defies the forgetfulness and loss inherent in both experience and writing (as if we could separate the pair), but
intensifies them until they turn round upon themselves to bring us to, and to
tell us what, we have always already forgotten—and that is intensity itself.
Eternity is something in the intensity of unknowing.

With Bataille as with Blanchot, we must remind ourselves that while it
is perhaps naive, it remains temptingly rational to think that we write in
order to *preserve*, to keep present. As Richard Stamelman writes in his analy-
sis of Jabès, in terms almost surprisingly appropriate to Bataille as well,

> There was once a time when it was believed that to put thoughts
> or feelings into words, to make them present and visible in the
> distinct shapes and dark lines of letters, assured their future. To
> write black on white was to give reality, if not immortality, to the
> shadowy, imprecise experiences of inner, subjective life. Writing
> was a means of halting the erosion of thought, feeling, and mem-
> ory caused by the passing of time. By inscribing words on a page,
> a writer was able to grasp permanently an elusive idea, to transfix
> a fleeting impression, and to seize an ephemeral perception before
> it disappeared.[2]

Here, I persist in thinking, is something which I am unwilling to lose,
and I set it down so that it may be re-presented in some future, when I am no
longer co-present with it. What will then be my past will have a new presence for another. Or perhaps I try to hold time fast just for myself: perhaps I
write against the fragility of my own memory. Set this down, I tell myself.
Write it now, before you lose it. That insurance against loss we suppose to be
the point: not to lose the present. Writing acts as guarantor of memory,
promising it for the future. Presence is thus reinforced against the steady erosion of time.

Less naively, we know that this takes both memory and writing a trifle
optimistically, pretending that the structure of temporality is not *essentially*
loss. When we write, it is not because we have nailed presence down but
because we have felt it slipping away, becoming the memory by which we
call to the absence that writing marks. As we have already seen in reading
Blanchot, writing's effort to manifest presence fails before the inescapable

conflict between presence and language. In that which language presents is the always-absence that is time.

We have already seen that we must link time to memory (memory, as I shall continue to argue, is all that we ever have of time), and if memory, as we like to hope, guards against the totality of loss, it is only by beginning in the constant loss which is the slippage of the present, a present always absent (slid away into the past) even as I set it down. We write against time, but time is writing's precondition. Attempting to carry a nonexistent present wholly into the future, writing empties itself of presence. I write to make a memory, forgetting that memory requires loss.

As if trying to slip across time, trying to slip the present past time, were not a sufficient impossibility, I must write as well past myself. I may write to the complications of myself in the future—to remind myself that I must do laundry, that I have to go to a meeting, that I have forgotten my umbrella. More commonly, I try to make of my memory another's future: I write to be read, write what (to recall yet another insight from Blanchot) I can never read.[3]

All of this takes place even when we think that we have understood: I know this, I think, and I write it down before I forget; I experienced this, I realize, and I write it down to let you know. We are perfectly well aware of flux and becoming, but we persist in clinging to the comforting falsity of the return of the identical; we set down what we can as if we thought it would really stay or at least come back, as if our writing could really say, *there* we have been, as if we were not lost in our language. As if the eternal return did not bring us to an infinite recirculation of loss. But all of this begs an important question: if writing does this anyway, why doesn't Bataille write like everyone else?

To approach an answer to this question, let us slip another set of problems into our writing. Let us suppose that we have never been there, and must write it nonetheless. Suppose that we must force through language not only the presence that language forgets, but that which can never have been present, the immemorial. What if there is nothing to remember, nothing but an already-given absence, the memory itself without an original—what if we suppose the absence of thing or self, knowing as we do that there must be a mutuality to this disappearance? What more must writing do to mark this distinctive absence, which begins, I think, as a matter of degree (all experience, passing through time, after all, entails some measure of loss) and finds its way into a difference in kind?

Or: what if the role of the forgotten in language is not undone but at once undone and intensified, in a preoccupation with the immemorial? What would define the immemorial in its divergence from the forgetting of "ordinary" experience; what would define the intensification of forgetting in language beyond its "ordinary" role, replaying the present/absent as memory; and, most centrally, why put into writing, as if to communicate it, the inherently unknowable, which (as Bataille says of all profound communication) demands silence?[4] I would suggest that in Bataillean terms the immemorial is already linked to, if not identified with, intensification to excess.

the immemorial inexperiencable

> Now dreams occurring in traumatic neuroses have the characteristic of repeatedly bringing the patient back into the situation of his accident, a situation from which he wakes up in another fright. This astonishes people far too little.
>
> —Sigmund Freud

In a way, Bataille's is an inversely but profoundly Freudian project. Like Bataille, Freud knew the complicity of the erotic and the deadly, and the deep memory of the immemorial. Consciousness, he tells us, is as much a filter as an openness to perception; consciousness, he tells us, is where in the ordinary sense we remember (where we remember what we know or knew); consciousness is where we find time (a notion he presents with a nod towards Kant).[5] But sometimes, as we have already noted in reading Blanchot, we "experience" the inexperiencable, the too-much, which is (whether in sensible or in affective terms) too violent for the filters of consciousness, too much at once—and this blind violence is something we never know; it rips straight through into the unconscious, where, free from the erosion of time, it pushes against consciousness. Unremembered, it repeats; when it breaks through, we do not recognize it. It comes to us only as memory, we were never there.

For Freud, the need to bring this violent immemorial moment, this moment we never forget (though neither can we recall it), to language is therapeutic. Repetition in his patients too often takes deeply discomfiting forms that do no one any good. But Bataille is not trying to heal himself (nor, for that matter, his readers). For Bataille, bringing to memory this blind immemorial moment does not mean taming the moment, as it does for the therapist (who tries to overcome the too-muchness). Thus Bataille must use his language differently, not to muffle this world-rending silence but to open the spaces in which it may resonate. For the therapist, we remember to *prevent* or to *end* the return of anguish. Memory becomes a way around silence, a way to avoid repetition. For Bataille, who taught the transformation of anguish to delight,[6] we replay, even in language, the possibilities of anguish, not to avoid or forget, but constantly to replay what we cannot hold in memory.

In such "experience" of the non-knowable, we face a difference in degree (of stimulation) which is at once a difference in kind: a (quantitative) too-much of stimulation that immediately renders transgressive (already crossed, then always uncrossed) the relation between unconscious and conscious (thus the quantitatively diverse becomes also qualitatively distinct). To call this "experience" is already problematic; it seems that we are dealing here with an intensity of stimulation that exceeds the possible grasp of an experiencing subject, but so far as I know, no better term is available. (Bataille further complicates matters by calling it "*inner* experience," though it must tear the subject out of itself.) This immediate crossing is the function of intensity, a philosophical focus which is Bataille's heritage from Nietzsche, certainly,[7] but also from Sade[8] and most probably, if less directly, from the medieval mystics as well. Intensification demands a new use of language. More precisely, it demands an intensification of what is inherent in language: the forgetfulness, the loss, the impossibility of writing. To burst discursive and systematic language, to foreground silence and impossibility, is not only to transgress but more strangely to intensify ordinary language—as communication, as transgressive intersubjectivity, as systematic rigor—so much that all of these functions turn around upon themselves and bring forth the impossible. It is this turning that I shall explore below.

We have some sense of how it is that Bataille introduces into language the slippage and discoherence that would seem to nullify, or to be nullified by, language. Foucault has nicely summarized these mechanisms:

> It is not only the juxtaposition of reflective texts and novels in the language of thought that makes us aware of the shattering of the philosophical subject. The works of Bataille define the situation in far greater detail: in the constant movement to different levels of speech and a systematic disengagement from the 'I' who has begun to speak . . . temporal disengagements . . . shifts in the distance separating a speaker from his words (in a diary, notebooks, poems, stories, meditations, or discourses intended for demonstration), an inner detachment from the assumed sovereignty of thought or writing (through books, anonymous texts, prefaces to his books, footnotes).[9]

To this we can add Bataille's own conscious emphasis on repetition: "One cannot . . . achieve the ultimate, except in repetition, for the reason that one

can never be sure of having attained it, that one can never be certain. . . ."[10]
Reading repetition we find ourselves uncertain whenever we think we know.
(Were we there, after all?)

Given this uncertainty, more, given his own decided emphasis on
unknowing and silence, the question becomes not "Why doesn't Bataille
write like other people?" but "Why does Bataille write at all?" Why does he
not keep silent, even if he cannot keep silence? It is here that the communicative insistence of the immemorial or unknowable (that is, of nonknowledge) comes into play.

the intensification of linguistic function

> The highest good and the highest evil are the same.
> —Friedrich Nietzsche

Written language in the "ordinary" sense (that is, discursive language that
presents information) attempts to communicate and to organize. Given the
tendency of silence to rupture order, we will not be surprised to find that
Bataille's effort to communicate silence makes for strange language. Silence
will not allow itself to be kept, nor is this merely an indication of our lack
of rigorous or ascetic self-discipline. It is not mere chatter that forces language open just where one would most expect, or most ask, that it keep
silent. Nor is it what Bataille calls the "little complacency" of discourse.[11] It
is other, more important, forces: the communicative insistence of the ecstatic, the rending pleasure of the violent, and the disciplinary demand of rigorous thought. Through these we can see why one must say what one cannot know.

Bataille tells us that his *inner experience*, his name for the "experience" of
the extreme (the erotic, the mystical), the most philosophically important,[12]
the ecstatic, the unknowable inexperiencable that tears one out of time—
that, the most defiant in the face of ordinary discourse—"is empty when
envisaged as a private exercise, only mattering for a single individual."[13] This
is so not only because we return to ourselves bursting with an overflow of joy
or an evangelical zeal (which is not to deny the possibility of either). At least
as significantly, *it*, the incommunicable, nevertheless demands communication at the very moment that it evades language. It is the immense alleluia
which is no less vital and violent, no less rupturing and rending, for being
"lost in endless silence."[14]

This demand works in both directions. That is: communication is neces-sary, not merely to keep the ecstatic from being an empty private project, but to attain to the ecstatic in the first place. "The extreme limit is elsewhere," Bataille writes; "It is only completely reached if communicated."[15] Yet "when the extreme limit is there, the means which serve to attain it are no longer there."[16] We attain to communication incompletely, only in laceration, in ripping apart our expressive, active, speaking, writing selves by expressing, acting, saying, writing too much. The means of communication, language among them, must intensify beyond their own limits, break open in and into silence. Language broken by silence maintains the open space of interroga-tion, the problematic rupture of the boundaries of the speaking subject.

Now, we must be careful not to think that in the annihilation of lan-guage we are somehow in a distinctly nonlinguistic realm. Pierre Klossowski is, as ever, eccentrically insightful on the nature of this language stripped of referential objectivity and fundamental stability:

> . . . to what does a language respond, whose propositions would no
> longer cause identities to intervene? It is no longer to being that
> a language liberated from all notions responds, abolishing itself
> with the identities; . . . being is no longer apprehended, other
> than as perpetually fleeing all that exists; in this sense, the notion
> claimed to circumscribe being, when it did nothing but obstruct
> the perspective of its flight. At last existence falls back into the
> discontinuous that it had never ceased to "be."[17]

Foucault is similarly perceptive, noting at once Bataille's need to keep lan-guage at a distance (lest its structure seem to stabilize discontinuity) and to throw himself into the space of language, in an effort to tear words apart: "Bataille's language . . . continually breaks down at the center of its space, exposing in his nakedness, in the inertia of ecstasy, a visible and insistent subject who had tried to keep language at arm's length, but who now finds himself thrown by it, exhausted, upon the sands of that which he can no longer say."[18] But these sands are a place to which only language can lead: "In effect, do we not grasp the possibility of such thought in a language which necessarily strips it of any semblance of thought and leads it to the very impossibility of language? right to this limit where the existence of lan-guage becomes problematic?"[19]

There is between language and silence an antagonism which is no less an inescapable mutuality. Transgression does not exist without boundaries, sac-rifice without victims, ecstasy without time. The more profoundly our com-munication demands silence, the more we must force open the way with words. Communication demands silence; silence demands words. It is silence's self-destructive expression, the word as the token of its own death,[20] that is so seductive. And seduction demands the maintenance of a certain shifting open space, of not quite expressible possibility.

What Bataille seeks from language is not a final, fully satisfactory explanation of the extreme, but we knew that, knowing an absence of need (even for meaning) to be more unfortunate than an absence of satisfaction.[21] Bataille in fact suggests that he may be writing precisely against that naive expectation with which I began this discussion:

> This is how I finally reach the end of language, which is death. Potentially the question's still one of language, but the meaning of this language (already meaning's absence) is implicit in words that put a stop to language. But these words acquire meaning only to the extent that they take place immediately before silence—a silence that puts a stop to them. Only *forgotten* would they take on full meaning. . . .[22]

Desire, even for meaning, is sustained; we get meaning only when we forget the words that would have meant. The function of Bataille's language is not to satisfy our desires but to intensify our needs: intensify them until their violence is adequate to the impossible task of ripping us out of ourselves, throwing us open to the impossible, a task of which, he tells us, only violence is capable. Death is not less violent for being still, nor the drive to death less destructive for working in silence. And the acquisition of meaning, where *meaning* belongs to silence and unknowing, can come about only in loss—in forgetting. As we have seen and shall again, Bataille is not the only thinker to make this extraordinary claim.

Bataille dramatically introduces fragmentation where we do not expect it, breaking sentences apart in the middle as if he forgot to finish them. The reader cannot gather meaning across the span of sentences and paragraphs into a satisfactory and satisfying understanding. We can only understand that this is language of elusion, that its forgetfulness is rigorous rather than sloppy or neglectful. In fact, its rigor attains to the stringency of violence.

Violence is silent, Bataille tells us, precisely in his discussion of Sade, who represents language pushed to its most violent extreme: ". . . since language is by definition the expression of civilized man, violence is silent. . . . *Violence is silent and de Sade's language is a contradiction in terms.* Common language will not express violence. . . ."[23] Sade seems to be the opposite of silent: he not only says, he repeats; he not only explains, he details as minutely as he possibly can. But this is not to deny the shifting unplaceable place of language in silence as much as of silence in language: "But silence cannot do away with things that language cannot state. Violence is as stubbornly there just as much as death, and if language cheats to conceal universal annihilation, the placid work of time, language alone suffers, language is the poorer, not time and not violence."[24] Somewhat unexpectedly, given the resolutely unpoetic nature of Sade's language, we find a link between the libertine language of debauchery and the pristine silence of poetry:

> What one doesn't grasp: that, literature being nothing if it isn't poetry, poetry being the opposite of its name, literary language— expression of hidden desires, of obscure life—is the perversion of language even a bit more than eroticism is the perversion of sexual function. Hence the "terror" which holds sway in the end "in letters," as does the search for vice, for new stimulation at the end of a debauchee's life.[25]

Like Sade, Bataille breaks the rules not by getting around them but by pushing them too far; his, too, is a pleasure in intensity that does not forego violence. (In the next chapter I shall have more to say about the peculiar relations of poetry itself to silence.)

The interdependence of language and silence, this demand for rules interplayed with breakage, is transgression's subtler aspect, too readily missed by those in love with the notion of flaunting their wild originality or of finding new boundaries to transgress. Here Bataille shares with Nietzsche the problem of appealing to the overenthusiastic and underdisciplined. Nietzsche's demand for the discipline of style is insistently rejected by the new disciples of Dionysus, as Bataille's love of rigorous method is cast aside by those too casually desirous of debasement. Silence demands not merely language, but (as Foucault notes) a rigorous language.[26] For Bataille, writing coheres only in the face of its imminent incoherence (forgetting, death, or disappearance): ". . . in everything I write there's the mark of death, of coming closer and closer to it (the only thing that gives my writing its coherence)."[27] But the converse is true as well: only writing as precise and rigorous as possible can really express the inexpressible, present the absent, remind us of what we can only have forgotten. Jean-Luis Baudry puts this rather better than I am able to:

> A methodological concern traverses the entire work of Bataille: to account for, to expose, and to build a knowledge of what is by nature inaccessible to knowledge. To measure up to the requirements of the heterogeneous, a heterogeneous doomed to silence

but which, if kept silent, would become the accomplice of repres-
sive homogenization. All of Bataille's practice in writing, in its
various forms, in its successive corrections and resumptions, aims
to respond to the existence of the heterogeneous by recognizing
that the discursivity of homogenizing thought has its rights, to
which it will not submit.[28]

To write explosions, we need explosives; explosive language needs something
to blow up. We recognize those rules of homogeneity to which we refuse to
submit; it is the violent consequences of insubmission that we seek.

To recognize and then to cross the rules is to transgress, seriously and
playfully at once:

> If transgression became the foundation-stone of philosophy . . .
> silent contemplation would have to be substituted for lan-
> guage. . . . Language has by no means vanished. How should one
> reach the heights if language did not point the way? but descrip-
> tive language becomes meaningless at the decisive instant when
> the stirrings of transgression itself take over from the discursive
> account of transgression, and one supreme moment follows these
> successive apparitions.[29]

Language, then, points the way (into a place we cannot go); it throws
into relief the silence that is its constant obverse. But there is more. Always
recognizing the impossibility of saying, Bataille persists, and he will not rest
with the relatively easy escape of purely negative claims. Thus, for example,
in his theory of religion, the extreme takes the name of the intimate, infinitely close and secretly shared:

> What is intimate, in the strong sense, is what has the passion of
> an absence of individuality, the imperceptible sonority of a river,
> the empty limpidity of the sky: this is still a negative definition,
> from which the essential is missing.
>   These statements have the vague quality of inaccessible dis-
> tances, but on the other hand articulated definitions substitute
> the tree for the forest, the distinct articulation for that which is
> articulated.
>   *I will resort to articulation nevertheless.* Paradoxically, intimacy is
> violence, and it is destruction, because it is not compatible with the
> positing of the separate individual. If one describes the individual in
> the operation of sacrifice, he is defined by anguish. But if sacrifice
> is distressing, the reason is that the individual takes part in it.[30]

If it is the anguish of sacrifice we must know, then let us know it not by the easy discursive distance of description, but by the sacrifice of language—sacrifice, transgression not in a "discursive account" but as these stirrings themselves. We do not recognize the shattering of the moment if we begin with discoherent pieces. "To shrink from fundamental stability isn't less cowardly than to hesitate about shattering it. . . . The more equilibrium the object has, the more *complete* it is, and the greater the disequilibrium of *sacrifice* that can result. These principles conflict with morality . . . they destroy the romantic morality of confusion as much as they do the opposite morality."[31] We need a language worth sacrificing: as complete as possible. Thus is intensified its sacrificial disequilibrium. Language in its sacrifice is not completeness and satisfaction but the lacerating incompletion of intolerable need: "The inevitable incompletion does not in any way delay the response, which is movement—were it in a sense the lack of a response. On the contrary, it gives it the truth of the impossible, the truth of a scream."[32]

how it sounds

> Words strain,
> Crack and sometimes break, under the burden,
> Under the tension, slip, slide, perish,
> Decay with imprecision, will not stay in place,
> Will not stay still.
>
> —T. S. Eliot

What speaks in Bataille's language is a Nietzschean religiosity not always distinguishable from a Sadean intensity: the convulsive ecstasy of the madness of God.[33] It is the madness of excess: ". . . that God whom we should like to shape into an intelligible concept never ceases, exceeding this concept, to exceed the limits of reason. In the domain of our life excess manifests itself insofar as violence wins over reason."[34] The madness of God is in no small part the constant interplay with humanity, the transgressive need of the sacred to cross over into profanity: "[One] pictures God himself succumbing to the desire for incompletion, the desire to be human and poor, and to die in torment."[35] Ultimately, "I become God, unknown, unknowable ignorance."[36]

Implicit in the madness of God, then, is the madness of humanity: I become God, and the profane recrosses the boundary of the sacred. We might in this connection recall these words which are not Bataille's but those of a man whose work he read with respect, worth introducing here just for a moment:

> Everything in the order of the written words which abandons the field of ordered and lucid perceptions; everything which aims at creating a reversal of appearances, to introduce doubt about the position of mental images and their relationship; everything which provokes confusion without weakening the burst of mental energy; everything which disrupts the relationships of things while giving this agitated mental energy an even greater aspect of truth and violence—all these offer death an exit, and relate us to certain most subtle states of the mind, at the heart of which death wants out.[37]

Antonin Artaud's are the words of a man institutionalized as mad, who insists that he is not mad but rather exceptionally self-aware: "I'm the man who's best felt the astounding disorder of his language in its relation to his thought. I am the man who has best charted his inmost self, his most imperceptible slitherings."[38] Not that this is an expression of self-satisfaction, for he also writes, "I'm an imbecile because of the suppression of thought, the malformation of thought. I'm empty because of the stupefaction of my tongue."[39] This emptiness of thought leads him frequently to the edge of the scream, to the truth Bataille likewise cherished; to a truth of flesh and, more particularly, blood, to inarticulate cries that matter exactly because they find their way into the most precise, lucidly terrifying discourse. It is the outcry of a man who, like Bataille, recognizes the curious fecundity of the void:

> I really felt that you were shattering the atmosphere around me, that you were creating a void in order to allow me to progress, in order to offer the expanse for an impossible space to that which within me was potentiality only, to a whole virtual germination that must be sucked into life by the interval which offered itself.
>
> Often I placed myself in this state of impossible absurdity in order to try and generate thought inside myself.[40]

We are as mad as the gods, and if we could properly say this, it would be in Artaud's broken voice that we would speak.

Artaud, facing impossibility, doubles the impossibility by demanding of time that it not only hold the present, but give him already the memory of the future: "I suspend this book in life; I'd like it to be bitten by external things,

and first of all by all the fits and starts, all the twitching *of my future self*."[41]
Bataille, who as the theoretician is the one who can tell us why we have
needed to break language further apart than ever, writes toward death; he
writes with the precision of a surgical scalpel; he slices time and saying open.
He will not forget: "I can henceforth not conceive of my life, if not pinned to
the *extreme limit of the possible*. (. . . But what to do? Forget? immediately, I
sense, I would go *mad*: one still understands poorly the misery of a mind
divested.")[42] But unforgetting, he will never know full meaning, for which forgetfulness is required. Desire is sustained. Bataille faces the impossible and
writes, because it is language that opens the possible: "When the power of
speech comes into the picture, the limit of possibility is the only limit."[43]

Bataille's language is far more conspicuously broken than Blanchot's; his
is fragmentation taken to a different extreme. His language, refusing to
cohere, brings us not knowledge but a vertiginous nonknowledge, opening as
certainly as Blanchot's to an outside of language to which language itself,
taken far enough, will inevitably bring us. Bataille's sentences do not gather
meaning across time but cut across themselves in time and meaning, opening
to an intensity where we never were, yet back toward which we are perpetually, seductively drawn. Only forgotten would they take on full meaning, stir-
ring beneath the conscious mind with redoubled force.

chapter three

*I*n the interrogative position: four poets

poetic madness

And in the end, in the expression which it is of itself, poetry is, necessarily, no less silence than language. Not through impotence. All of language is given to it as is the strength to engage it. But silence intended not to hide, not to express at a higher degree of detachment. Experience cannot be communicated if the bonds of silence, of effacement, of distance, do not change those they put into play.

—Georges Bataille

Associations both ancient and contemporary link poetry to the historical silence of madness. Plato has Socrates alternately praise and decry the work of the poets on just this ground. In the *Republic*, poetic madness is a dangerous mode to enter or to imitate, lest it malform the souls of its readers.[1] Yet in the *Phaedrus*, Socrates praises the divine madness of the poet as much as of the lover. Here madness is linked as well to the opening of the future: "The people who designed our language in the old days never thought of madness as something to be ashamed of or worthy of blame; otherwise they would not have used the word 'mania' for the finest experts of all—the ones who tell the future—thereby weaving insanity into prophecy."[2] In this dialog the variant which is poetic madness is described as "possession by the Muses," of which Socrates warns, "If anyone comes to the gate of poetry and expects to become an adequate poet by acquiring expert knowledge of the subject without the Muses' madness, he will fail, and his self-controlled verses will be eclipsed by

the poetry of men who have been driven out of their minds."[3] This sits oddly
with Socrates' more frequent and more famous praise of both rationality and
self-control, but this complicated figure is, as Phaedrus himself notes, "not at
home" in this discussion of love, poetry, and other modes of madness.[4] This
may well be so, not because Socrates is in some manner deficient, but because
poetry is itself unsettling and necessarily takes us, any "us," away from being
at home.

In our own day Blanchot, as we have seen, draws the madness of poetry
into this same future opening; for him, though, the future opens not onto
prophecy but, like all writing in the *Phaedrus*, onto unanswerable questions.[5]
With Nietzsche, he suggests that we love our ignorance of the future (our lack
of answers, which maintains questioning); strictly speaking, we maintain the
word *madness* in the interrogative position, the position of poetry. Hölderlin
was mad, but was he? Poetry, like madness, turns language to its own interrogation; it turns our talkative breath back upon silence, as Celan tells us.[6] It
calls back to an "original," but the original is beyond memory, beyond hav-
ing-been-there. Future silence, of course, includes that of which we are most
deeply ignorant, the secret and the unanswerable, death as well as madness.
When the poet turns the question of language toward the space of the sacred,
the nonanswer of the future (the ignorance that one loves) turns back too
upon an anteoriginal silence (a rupture across which love draws us, as later
chapters will show), and the question of poetry becomes the interrogation of
language itself, of human and divine, word and Word alike. Four such poets
of both silence and the sacred will come under exploration here, two from the
Judaic and two from the Christian tradition: Friedrich Hölderlin, Rainer-
Maria Rilke, Paul Celan, and Edmond Jabès.

It is perhaps Hölderlin and Celan among these who are most conspicuously poets of silence, poets whose lines break without forming sentences,
whose words open most obviously onto their own incompletion. But it was not
only of himself that Celan spoke when he said in his 1960 acceptance of the
Büchner prize, which has come to be called the Meridian speech, "the poem
today shows—and this has only indirectly to do with the difficulties of vocabulary, the faster flow of syntax, or a more awakened sense of ellipsis, none of
which we should underrate—the poem clearly shows a strong tendency toward
silence."[7] Hölderlin and Rilke famously precede and, if anyone could be said
to do so, influence Celan; Jabès too, following him, tends toward silence,
writes of the particular silence of the book itself. For each, language is the per-
formance of multiple interrogations; silence is the withdrawal of multiple
kinds of meanings. And time itself turns, returns, and vanishes in the name,
the text, again, in human and divine alike. Behind each and all of these

absences, before and after each of these silences, is a peculiarly divine silence, the "original poem" (which is never first), the silent poem unfallen from which the writing of poetry may yet derive an emergent grace.

Jabès

> From the depths of sedentary existence a nomadic memory arises.
> —Emmanuel Levinas

We begin with the silence of the text itself.

In Edmond Jabès's remarkable works, structures and stories derived from both Talmudic and Hassidic traditions frame an absent God, indeed a God of paradigmatically Jewish absence—absent no more importantly from the world than from the book, the word. "God withdrew from the world, not to settle man there, but the word."[8] This is a God who is by now not unfamiliar, or whose necessary unfamiliarity is by now familiar to us; the God who by the generosity of withdrawal leaves the space of creation, for creation. And yet this space is not left altogether, in Jabès's reading: "He knew the latter would automatically arrogate the right to annex the universe. Also, he could not bring himself to renounce his kingdom altogether."[9]

The word, then, may well mark the absence of God, but there is always some unrenounced trace of divinity within it—and an insistence upon reaching out to encompass, even, the divine. Indeed language is our sole approach from the temporal profane to the eternal sacred: "God is his word, and this living word must forever be rewritten. The believing Jew cannot go toward God except through the Book, but the commentary on the original Text is not a commentary on the divine Word."[10] The silence of *that* Word eludes us. Its echo in our words remembers us to where we never were, to the "outside time, the time of the book at its prelude . . . echo smothered by echo."[11] It remembers us before us, and yet it gestures beyond and after us. Outside the horizontal linearity of time, past and future become oddly similar:

> Memory means the promise of a future. "Tell me what you remember, and I shall tell you who you will be," wrote Reb Horel, one of the imaginary rabbis. . . .
>
> "Can we remember a place where we have not been, a face we have not come near, an object we have never held?" Reb Zaoud asked Reb Bécri.

"I well remember God," replied the latter.[12]

And again:

"But this after-death is also a before-death . . . like memory,
as if there were always something before."[13]

We write, it seems, where we do not quite remember (or where remembering becomes so transformed as to call to the future); we write toward the call of silence, where we never were. ". . . [W]hat continues to be written here," Jabès writes, what continues rather than ever being begun, "is written in a past I cannot vouch for, a past which, however, was a continuous present up to the decisive break I cannot place in time because I have no memory or words left and, in the place where I am still, with more and more difficulty, trying to move, there is no time."[14] This decisive break, I suspect, comes before and after and outside of all time; it is the place which cannot be placed in time because it is the very placement of time, the memory of a no-place where there is no time—a place not altogether unlike the Socratic unmoving/circling of the Gods which the *Phaedrus* presents as the perfect abode of the soul, or the Freudian unconscious into which the too-much of the immemorial withdraws. But it is not precisely either one. It is the memory of the well-remembered God, or perhaps it is no memory at all. It is without the words by which we customarily tag our memories. It is the forgotten remembrance that has withdrawn itself from words, in order that there may be words, as from the world, that it may be at all.

The word may mark the absence of God, but the trace of unrenounced divinity in it remembers timelessness to us. Jabès writes of the "[p]urity of silence! Not of the silence that knows, that has listened and repeated, but of the silence that has forgotten."[15] Silence has forgotten, the word remembers, but it is called to remember beyond itself, to forget itself in silence. What's more, we're told, "God speaks in oblivion. His word means forgetting. It is a word of forgetting, forgetting all words."[16] Forgetting becomes the possibility of our speaking as well: "And can we infer that silence is forever the echo of a first silence, that of the divine Word perceived at its borders of oblivion? As if only oblivion were audible?"[17] Audible oblivion (also a pledge of the future) echoes this originary forgetful word. Like Bataille, then, Jabès suggests that meaning demands forgetfulness, indeed that forgetfulness lies behind the very possibility of hearing anything from which meaning might be gathered. Like Blanchot, he suggests that forgetfulness may be primary.

Jabès's sense of God's absenting-creating word is perhaps an unusual twist upon Genesis, the words of which will be turned again by the Hellenic Christianizing of John. In Genesis, of course, it is by speaking that God makes:

"And God said, 'Let there be light,' and there was light," and so too for the creation of sky, water, land, vegetation, heavenly bodies, nonhuman living creatures, and finally human beings.[18] "In the beginning," says John, much later, "was the Word." Is this not contradictory of Jabès's take on the tradition? "And the Word was with God, and the Word was God."[19] Surely this Christian reinterpretation opposes the withdrawal of God as the settling of the word in the world? Perhaps, though, it is in absenting himself that God speaks; perhaps creation is the withdrawal of a Word which is, paradoxically, also a silence so infinite that it would destroy us, a silence that bewitches fatally our desire to speak: "Man," warns Jabès, "has no *need* for the infinite. . . . It is our thoughts, words, vocabularies, always attempting to go beyond, that are fatally bewitched by it."[20]

What's more, in the beginning, as Augustine (we shall see) sternly reminds us, there is time. The word as the placement of God in time is also a word in time *as* time itself (congruent, after all, with the customary reading of *Word* as Christ, a God in time in the deep paradox of the incarnation). That is, the word makes time; time is the beginning, the beginning of beginnings and endings. It is with God but it is the absence of God, the absence of and with eternal presence in an infinite passing of time. In the beginning, God speaks, and it is good—but then, in speaking God is gone, looking on from afar, absent from the word as the word remains in time, present only in the timelessness of the Word, the trace of eternity in time. His word means forgetting of all words, the atemporality "prior" to all creation.

This withdrawn God is gone from our time and from our words, too. We shall have occasion when we turn to more explicitly theological writers to discuss more fully the fallenness of our language, a fallenness curiously of concern to all of these poets, devotees of language themselves. Ours is after all a language bound to time, only comprehensible in time. "Readability—of the book—depends upon the time—of the book," writes Jabès.[21] And though this bookish time is, as Blanchot has already warned us, no ordinary time (it may even be destructive of coherent linear time), readability lies outside of eternity, in time, even if it is the reiterated time of the book. The word in time may be bewitched by the silence it breaks and cannot understand: "Undeciphered book of God within the decoded book of man, where every word, bathed in wounded silence, mimics the agony of an original word whose oblivion could only be the blank space of its divine destiny, silence at its confines, lagging behind infinite silence."[22]

Silence pervades our texts, silence and forgetting. Our words murmur with the memory of forgetfulness itself, the outside of time where we have never been. Jabès tells us of silence and absence, both bewitching the presence of finite, graspable meaning. But we need the finite, the spoken and the written, in order to reach toward the infinity which may be fatal to us. For Jabès as for Bataille, we need words to break.

> The Word of God has been silent since the day when, in order to be heard, He enjoined silence on our human words, forgetting that it was through them that He spoke to us.
>
> The silence of the Word of God is but the infinite silence of our crushed, common words.
>
> We cannot attain the silence of God except by making it our own. Recognizing the Word of God would then mean accepting our own silence.
>
> To say this silence means to say the sacred, but also, at the same time, to undo it.[23]

This said-and-undone silence is a complex silence, a speaking of our own echoing a divine silence, a silence of God's which is inseparable from both divine and human words. The very name of God, Jabès says, "is always a word before or after words, a word without words, past or future, a futile word whose use shocks the mind."[24] But

> "If God Himself is an absent word, or rather, absence of words,
>   then is not every vocable a carbon of this absence?"
> Exploitation of absence: divine language.
> You write on God.[25]

All writing writes into the silence from which it came. It is "an act of silence directed against silence,"[26] a positive gesture, but one which threatens blasphemy in every invocation of the sacred. Silence, too, like the absence of God, has an unexpected positivity, even as it likewise calls to an infinite, ungratifiable, fatal desire. Indeed, desire itself has joyful names.

For Jabès, the brokenness or incompletion of human language, its fragmentation by silence, is at the same time its gift: silence makes possible the spaces of both interrogation and desire. Interrogation is for Jabès a fundamental relation between human and divine as well as between human speakers. He explicitly connects his own poetry with Blanchot's theorizing:

> . . . it was Blanchot who noticed this . . . when two people talk, one of them must always remain silent. . . . If we both spoke at the same time, neither one of us could hear what the other was saying. Now, during this silence that you impose on yourself, you are all the

while forming questions and answers in your mind. . . . And as I
continue to speak, you are eliminating questions from your mind:
ah, you say to yourself, that's what he meant, all right. But what if I
went on speaking for a long time and we went away before you had
a chance to reply? When we met again, you wouldn't come back
with an answer; you would come back with a question.[27]

Or, as Richard Stamelman nicely puts it in "Nomadic Writing: The poetics of
exile," "The aphorism's self-contained completeness and classical perfection are
misleading. Jabès's aphorism is not an answer but a perpetually open and
reopened question."[28] Jabès gives us not self-contained units but, like both Blanchot and Bataille, deliberately broken fragments. And, as I have remarked, the
interrogation inherent in the fragment is always addressed to the divine as well:

> All questions are first of all questions put to God.
> Around the Word of the desert, displacement became an
> implacable interrogation. As if it were up to thought to trace in
> the long and difficult path toward the supreme truth which our
> eager truths run up against. Supreme Truth as blinding untruth or,
> rather, as One-and-Only Truth, a stranger to any Truth it denies.
> Truth risen from the ashes of our powerless mortal truths: its name
> is *a splendid negation of name*.[29]

This perpetual interrogation, this negation of all names, this infinite
refusal of God to resolve into a stable present, is also itself desire, a desire
which like Bataille's is directed elsewhere than its own satisfaction. As Edward
Kaplan puts it, "Belief inhibits the constant flow of desire. For Jabès, doubt
preserves desire. . . . Jabès then revises the notion of biblical revelation. Writing is a refusal of the given. . . ."[30] Post-Hegelian French tradition, particularly
through Kojève (not coincidentally, Bataille attended Kojève's lectures),
equates desire with the refusal of the given; desire is always for something
other, or more. Desire is worth preserving; it is more important than satisfaction. Like Blanchot, Jabès sees joy and disaster as intertwined; like Bataille, as
going beyond themselves, where desire draws forth our exiled words.

Celan

Remember, beware of forgetfulness and yet, in that faithful memory, never will you know.
                                                —Maurice Blanchot

Paul Celan confronts an absence more immediate and confounding in its fini-
tude than even the absence of the names of God. He confronts an absence of
human meaning—the destruction of both human and humane—after
Auschwitz, when it may well be, contrary to Adorno, that we can write *only*
poetry,[31] when we must fill our language with the silence that will break our
words along with our selves. Yet in his work a number of themes parallel those
of Jabès: not only the emphasis on silence, but also the concern with forgetfulness in language and before language, with the absent origin of the poem;
with death and loss but also with memory and a dark desiring hope; with
questions as all that remain to us of speaking. Celan's poetry is not an attempt
to restore or even re-find meaning, as if we could make up in words for the
Holocaust, but to get beyond meaning, to get before and after it, to write, as
bodies write in *Engführung*, "asunder" (*auseinandergeschrieben*), in a place
which seems to have a name, but has none—a splitting asunder which eludes
the word's ability to name.[32]

Celan's poetry has been not infrequently accused of hermeticism, but it
is its very silence which makes his work anything but hermetic—silence
which, far from surrounding and sealing off each poem, tears through his
poems, cuts open his language. Celan himself refused the label "hermetic":
"[In] Katherine Washburn's introduction to her translation of Celan . . . she
cites Celan's inscription (presented to Michael Hamburger) stating that he
was 'ganz und gar nicht hermetisch [certainly not hermetic].'"[33] Too many critics have read his silence as a failing, as undesirable, even reductive. Bianca
Rosenthal summarizes some of these criticisms in regard to a 1968 work: "Karl
Krolow . . . saw *Fadensonnen* [Threadsuns] as Celan's endeavor to realize the
impossible . . . in this particular volume through his representation of 'des
"singbaren Rests" von Sprache.' [the 'singable remnants' of speech]. The dan-
gerously narrow language edge that Celan was always walking became
increasingly more so . . . and could easily be reduced to silence. . . . Rudolf
Hartung [also] placed *Fadensonnen* 'an der Grenze zum Schweigen' [at the
border of silence]."[34]

This narrow edge, though, this border is not something simply crossed. It
is an edge that cuts open language, like the "prayer-sharp knives" of silence,
cutting, as prayer is meant to do, across the limit of the profane.[35] Such sharp-
edged silence is far from reductive. Like the cut, it multiplies surfaces and
depths, multiplies language and its possibilities.[36] There is little question that
Celan is, often explicitly, a poet of silence. But, as Leonard Olschener writes,

> One of the most consequential paradoxes surrounding Paul
> Celan's work, one allied to its patent resistance to a feared adul-

teration by misused, euphemistic, and outworn, obsolete metaphorical language, originates in the silence from which his poetry emanates, the silences inherently belonging to Celan's sense of language. To be sure, this situation does not pertain to Celan uniquely—Hölderlin and Rilke, both formative influences, paradigmatically faced related problems—but his work came early on to be associated with *Verstummen*, as though this reductive term, taken alone, were an insightful and hence hermeneutically productive label.[37]

Celan's is not silence which is simply unable to speak, forced to muteness. Rather it is a silence which is intercut with language and mutually complicated by it.

After Auschwitz, there *must be* poetry, in which language is torn and broken, into which words are pulled, but in which there is also an essential address: the words and the silences are pulled toward an other. The openness reminds us of the conversational silences of which Blanchot writes, the interrogative speech which for Jabès is all of human speaking. "A poem," Celan said at Bremen, "being an instance of language, hence essentially dialogue, may be a letter in a bottle thrown out to sea with the—surely not always strong—hope that it may somehow wash up somewhere, perhaps on the shoreline of the heart. In this way, too, poems are *en route*: they are headed toward. Toward what? Toward something open, inhabitable, an approachable you, perhaps. . . ."[38] But poetry addresses no easy or comforting words in its approach to such a 'you,' nor to any other. It does not inquire comfortably; it asks but it does not ask after you (Nowhere/ does anyone ask after you).[39] It asks but does not ask after; it interrogates radically. Nor does it reach that other toward whom it goes: "It is lonely," says Celan; "Its author stays with it."[40] Like Lenz shouting "Long live the king," the poem, Celan tells us, ". . . is a terrifying silence. It takes his—and our—breath away. Poetry is perhaps this: an *Atemwende*, a turning of our breath. Who knows, perhaps poetry goes its way—the way of art—for the sake of just such a turn?"[41]

Why this turn? Perhaps because, breathless and terrified, we must turn back, not to an answer but, lonely still, to all we have: to the fact that we can still ask questions, still ask for answers. "The poem holds its ground, if you will permit me yet another extreme formulation, the poem holds its ground in its own margin. In order to endure, it constantly calls and pulls itself back from an 'already-no-more' into a 'still-here.' This 'still-here' can only mean speaking. Not language as such, but responding. . . ."[42] Responding: not answering with a sense of finality (finally giving the True name), but drawing toward, being drawn toward the spaces between words; not language as such, but the very possibility of response, the very necessity of interrogation. "The poem intends another, needs this other, needs an opposite. It goes toward it, bespeaks it."[43] "The poem," says Celan, "becomes . . . desperate conversation," a conversation that creates its addressee by being conversation (that is, by being the possibility of response).[44] It is a conversation which nonetheless violates the silence that is (as we saw with Blanchot) both its precondition and its destruction, a conversation after all meaning, "the wounding of syntax, the cutting agony of language itself."[45] The addressee is not the topic of the inquiry—nowhere does anyone ask after you—but rather serves as the space of possible interrogation, the space that lets us turn back and ask. Silence, we recall, is also an interrogation. It is the very possibility of interrogation, up to the limit of meaning, beyond the limit where it becomes madness, a future so open that it breaks outside time, so that time turns back toward an absent origin.

Indeed, the addressee may nearly be identified with this space of silence, with the trace of humanity left in silence. The addressee may personify this interrogative space: "only the space of this conversation can establish what is addressed, can gather it into a 'you' around the naming and speaking I. But this 'you,' come about by dint of being named and addressed, brings its otherness into the present."[46] Whatever I may say, it will be too much speaking, as if the interrogation could only find perfection in the absence of the answer, the answer which is itself perhaps absence or at least the space of otherness, a space which tells us that naming has withdrawn:

> And the too much of my speaking:
> heaped up around the little
> crystal dressed in the style of your silence.[47]

Faced with the absence of meaning, we yet cannot keep silent; silence cannot be kept. If we cannot quite remember, the poem at least reminds us of this:

> The silicified saying in the fist,
> you forget that you forget,
>
> blinking, the punctuation marks
> crystallize at the wrist,
>
> . . . there, by
> the sacrifice-bush,
> where memory catches fire, . . .[48]

If horror as well as joy has left us the space of the immemorial, we can at least remember that we have forgotten. At least, that is, we can remember forget-fulness itself, where

> a strange lostness was
> palpably present, almost
> you would
> have lived.[49]

Almost, Celan writes, *beinah*, nearly. Almost alive, almost present. As we shall see again, distance plays here against proximity.[50] The "almost" opens onto a subjunctive (you *would* have lived), a space of loss to which our words call us, calling toward their own silencing, their palpably present loss. *Almost*, as we shall see again, does not imply a proximity either spatial or temporal, as if life were right next door or a few minutes later or earlier, but a proximity of sustained nearness/ farness, a prolonged seductive evocation, a drawing-forth.

Silence for Celan is as sharp as both blasphemy and prayer.[51] Words are guilty, almost criminal:

> What times are these
> when a conversation
> is almost a crime
> because it includes
> so much made explicit?[52]

They are scapegoats for our guilt:

> They discharge the guilt that adhered to their origin,
> they discharge it upon a word
> that wrongly subsists, like summer.[53]

The guilt is that of postlapsarian language, language fallen beyond the possi-bility that it might find salvation in the simple refusal to speak. In Celan's poetry, names call out. But they seldom call to specific, reachable addressees. (To approach you, after all, is not yet to reach you.) They call to the absence of any answer.

Silence, I have suggested, tears open, ruptures Celan's poetry rather than hermetically surrounding it. Yet it is true too that the poem is surrounded by silence. It reaches out around itself, in time, into silence, reaches both for-ward and back for what is unreadable within it. Like Jabès's, Celan's poetry seeks both a past beyond origin and a future beyond answer. Bianca Rosenthal interprets Harald Weinrich's remarks on Celan in 1963's *Lexikon der Weltliteratur*: "Weinrich discerned no signs of a turning point in *Atemwende*. If anything, he wrote, there is a strong inward tendency toward an imaginary point where the absolute poem originates. Celan submits to this demand, which Mallarmé was the first to claim for modern poetry, and he attempts 'Mallarmé konsequent zu Ende denken' (to think Mallarmé consistently to the end)."[54] But this absolute origin must also be an originary absence, and it will not present itself where we expect it: "Celan's work also includes language and poetry coming from silence and loss of speech, from memory and oblivion. . . . Celan, according to [Kurt] Oppens, was already a dead man when he appeared on his poetic stage. His poetry is a process of resurrection. . . ."[55]

The origin of the poem, then, is a re-origin, a resurrection after an "original" loss prior to any possession. It thus requires this loss as much as its restoration. Aris Fioretos writes, ". . . indeed, it would be far from wrong to consider Celan's poetry to be inscribed between the poles of extinction and survival. In this poetry, at once painful memory and shivering novelty, an experience of the limits of language is rendered evident."[56] I would suggest only that the first pole of Celan's poetry is less survival than rebirth, always again and always caught up in loss already. Fioretos adds, "Language is the medium of remembrance, but a medium which does not interiorize the remembered so much as it repeats it figuratively."[57] Celan's is more literally than most a language of memory; much of his poetry is written in German at a time when he no longer habitually speaks or is surrounded by it, during his life in France. Language is always a repetition; it has its origin in loss. The poem reaches "toward something open," not a fixed point of either memory or otherness, but perhaps toward that opening of the (absent) "original" poem. Yet surely this reaching back is a turning, a turning point or gesture, toward a perhaps unfallen silent poem, without guilt, without the guilt that adheres to word-corpses.

A corpse that almost would have lived. Christopher Fynsk reminds us of the interplay of proximity and distance, in that *almost*, in Celan's poetry: "Still, silence and the din of 'murderous speech' remark a kind of presence of language itself . . . language remaining, persisting in its nearness. . . . An effort, then, to bring a mute language into speech (but in its muteness), to work in its *proximity*, and to bring forth from this proximity (which is also a distance) what language still offers of relation. . . ."[58] Interrogation may invite and be invited by the other, but it does not bring that other near; it opens an uncloseable space in which otherness, other times and other-than-time, makes its way toward presence. And so too the poem "presents" the eternal, the other of time, time's outside, in its silence. That "original" silence is only the palpable presence of loss, the murmur of *almost*, nearby but never here: as if language were unfallen, as if we had forgotten and the grass had grown together rather than being written asunder, as if writing did not cut apart, as if someone, somewhere, asked after you, as if you knew the Name by which to ask after the infinite.

But it is the eternal, the infinite, the proximate divine 'you' that we can no longer call by name, nor perhaps ever could. Christianity and Judaism alike suggest, if in different ways, that we cannot; each refuses to God the name, though naming was to have been a divine gift to humanity. Adam could name what surrounded him but not what excluded him, the world but not his God. The Old Testament God declares austerely "I am," and in fact strict Jewish tradition often forbids the use of a name for God. The New Testament Christ calls out on the cross to a relation ("my God") but not to a name (I shall recur to this point in the final chapter). If naming occurs in the depths of language,[59] perhaps the nameless is at the deepest end of silence. And perhaps it is this particular un-naming which argues for the fall of language, for the truth of a fallen language. Celan's *almost* echoes an earlier forgetting, Augustine's, which will be important for us soon. I don't know, says Blanchot, but I have the feeling I'm going to have known. Celan gives to us the feeling that we will already have forgotten. If there is hope in this poetry, it is for the open space, the question, not the answer but the very possibility of response, a possibility sustained in silence.

Hölderlin

Something was there, which has now gone. Something has disappeared. How can I retrieve it and look over my shoulder towards what comes before, if all my power consists in turning it into what comes after? The language of literature is a quest for this moment that precedes it.

—Maurice Blanchot

As the associations with divinity suggest, silence may connote reverence as much as failure in language. Friedrich Hölderlin is often cited as an influence on Celan, as one of the first poets for whom silence becomes an explicit preoccupation. His is not a poetry which has to contend with the world after

Auschwitz (he died in 1843), but the secularity he faces, the difficulty of being a poet who seeks oneness with all in a fragmented world, nonetheless resonates well into the next centuries. Hölderlin's is a more overtly joyous silence than we have seen before:

> Him, the most High, shall I name then? A God does not love what's unseemly,
> Him to embrace and hold our joy is too small.
> Silence often behooves us: deficient in names that are holy,
> Hearts may beat high, while the lips hesitate, wary of speech?[60]

It is clear that this "deficiency" is a testimony to awe and delight; indeed, "our joy is too small," perhaps because as *our* joy it is reduced to the bounds of subjectivity. It would be unseemly to reduce this already-too-small joy to the still-smaller containment of words. Yet the poem itself is words, of course, and it is words here which tell us that often we must fall silent. It seems that for Hölderlin what is sacred may be the very space of this lack of names, of silence: "I understood the silence of Aether," he tells us, "But human words I've never understood./ . . . I grew up in the arms of the Gods."[61] The Gods at home, it seems, are silent; perhaps silence often behooves us in respectful imitation of them.

For Hölderlin, too, silence stands as a rupture of origin. By this phrase I would imply both its function as interrogation—the rupture in language which first opens the space by which speaking and writing are made possible—and that elusive sense of an "original" unfallen silence, in quotations as our "origin" because this is where we never were. For Hölderlin language not only is temporal, but may even be what draws us into time. (Hence language is unseemly in praise of the eternal Gods.) Time and language are blessed, it seems, by their drawing-in of eternal silence:

> How dear to us you were in silence there
> You, priestess, lived and guarded the sacred flame,
> Yet dearer now, amid the time-bound
> Blessing the times by your celebration.[62]

Hölderlin's is often poetry of celebration and praise, yet what is praised may be in problematic relation to the time of praising. This is true even where the figure being praised is human. Hölderlin writes in "Bonaparte," "In the poem he cannot live and last;/ He lives and lasts in the world."[63] It is as if the poem performed the reverse of its traditional commemorative, immortalizing function, as if it only sped the temporal passage. Hölderlin's poetry expresses the hope of a new time, a time outside the constraints of time, but the fulfillment of this hope remains perpetually uncertain. He praises Princess Augusta of Hamburg, hoping "that this joyful day would initiate/ For me a new time also. . . ."[64] Perhaps the "fulfillment" of poetry's hope is an open space of perpetual desire, another suspended openness outside of time.

Words fail before what is wonderful. Even Christ seems in Hölderlin's work to fall short of words in the face of goodness. In a fragmentary version of "Patmos," Hölderlin writes:

> And in his great soul, carefully choosing, the lord
> Pronounced death, and the ultimate love, for never
> He could find words enough
> To say about kindness, then, and to affirm the affirmative.

A disturbing implication soon follows: "Yet this he recognized. All is good. Thereupon he died."[65] It is as if the recognition of goodness were sufficient for death—or perhaps it is all we need of living? The earlier, more complete version of "Patmos" makes a still stronger gesture toward the insufficiency of language:

> For all things are good. After that he died. Much could
> Be said of it. And the friends at the very last
> Saw him, the gladdest, looking up triumphant.[66]

Much could be said, but it is not. Much could be said, but could it?

The time of these poems is a time reaching toward timelessness, as their language is a reaching toward wordless spaces, spaces still open, where much could be said, but is not; is not, perhaps, in order to keep the openness itself. The time of this poetry reaches before and after into eternities of still spaces. Hölderlin's yearning for a "past" extends well beyond his idyllic sense of childhood, important though that often is for him. Tenses intertwine, as Eckart Förster writes: "only those who can recollect are able to foresee. For foresight is not a mere apprehension of future events; rather we are always anticipating the future in relation to what lies in wait for it. This is why foresight is always the foresight of something soon to be past, and so of a recollection to come. And to this extent the inner form of memory does not restrict it to an apprehension of what was."[67]

Memory thus calls to no simple past. "[Hölderlin] saw remembrance as bound up with the essence of poetry. . . ."[68] Time itself seems to turn back, as in "The Ister":

> Yet almost this river seems
> To travel backwards and
> I think it must come from
> The East.
> Much could
> Be said about this. And why does
> It cling to the mountains, straight?[69]

The river seems to travel easterwards, almost, back before itself to a prior resurrection, and much could be said, but, again, is not; again, this "much"
opens straight onto a question, onto another opening.

David Constantine rightly says of Hölderlin's poetry, "the dynamism is
that of an insatiable longing."[70] It is, in fact, a longing back before and well
beyond the speaking, writing self, a longing taken to divine proportions.
Hölderlin's poetry reaches back not only to a preverbal infancy, but to a
prelapsarian silent grace. The Gods and their silences are alike absent, and
we cannot call them by name. "Germania" calls only to the absence:

> Gods who are fled! And you, also, present still,
> But once more real, you had your time, your ages!
> No, nothing here I'll deny and ask no questions.[71]

There are no questions—no interrogation that would draw the Gods to us. I
have already noted that for Hölderlin language seems, where it reaches to
silence, to draw silence too into time; so, too, in the always-double interrogative pull (despite the emphatic set of negatives, Hölderlin poses questions
always), silence may pull our words into eternity.

> For once, however, even a God may choose
> Mere daily tasks, like mortals, and share all manner of fate.
> This is a law of fate, that each shall know all others
> That when the silence returns there shall be a language too.[72]

Gods in the world return like silences in language, as openness, as possibility
within fate.

In the beginning, in our beginning, is still the word, even if it remains
somehow distant from us:

> A stranger it comes
> To us, that quickening word,
> The voice that moulds and makes human.[73]

The creative word is as much a stranger to us as inhuman, aethereal silence. And yet the stranger's distance will play off human proximity in an approach without contact. Interiority will play off the outside, where a heart of silence and the absence of meaning burst words from within. If the quickening word comes from the home of the Gods, it is pervaded by silence. It is not simply fallen chatter, though neither, if we hear it, can it be wholly unfallen. In the poem "As on holiday," Hölderlin's "false priest" has been cast down by heaven, and while it may be despair which breaks his speech, it seems too that his words fragment into silence just where the mnemonic pull of the divine is strongest:

> . . . yet in the far-flung down-rushing storms of
> The God, when he draws near, will the heart stand fast.
> But, oh, my shame! when of
>
> My shame!
>
> And let me say at once
>
> That I approached to see the Heavenly,
> And they themselves cast me down, deep down,
> Below the living, into the dark cast down
> The false priest that I am, to sing,
> For those who have ears to hear, the warning song.
> There[74]

What we have to hear is not the silence of the Gods, but the priest's song of warning. Here too the infinite may be fatal to us. "There"—the poem ends without completion by word or even punctuation. "There," much could be said, perhaps, or not. Approaching the heavenly, sentences do not cohere. Words break.

Intensity, we recall—joy and despair alike—may burst time to eternity. Silence bursts language *there*. There, where we find ourselves drawn, both before and after as these burst out of *now*. In despair, to be sure:

> By that mysterious yearning toward the chasm;
> Chaotic deeps attract, and whole peoples too
> may come to long for death . . .[75]

But too, in a move Rilke will come to share with him, Hölderlin celebrates the singular ecstatic moment that suffices to eternity, the intensity of the "now" which is enough for an ever: "For *once* I / Lived, like the Gods, and no more is needed."[76] Like Rilke too, Hölderlin demands attention, which Celan calls the "natural prayer of the soul,"[77] attention to things, to speak of which is altogether seemly:

> . . . but what the Father
> Who reigns over all loves most
> Is that the solid letter
> Be given scrupulous care, and the existing
> Be well interpreted.[78]

The care given to the word, the "solid letter" of the word, and the existing thing seem to be the same. Or, more exactly, there is a close alliance between our scrupulous attention to both, different though they are, the existing and the written. And this attention, it seems, is pleasing to the Gods, who perhaps can share it only through us, can only in our praise of the world attend from eternity to a single word, a thing, a now.

This attentive care, Rilke will later suggest, is the one thing we have to say to the divine. Intensifying by this natural prayer a single moment, we share the power of the Gods: not to make the moment last forever, but to take it outside time. Eternity is something intensive about time, not something extensive.

We cannot say divinity; *Es fehlen heilige Namen*, names for the holy are lacking. But we can wrap our guilty words around the temporal moment:

> For once between Day and Night must
> A truth be made manifest.
> Now threefold circumscribe it,
> Yet unuttered also, just as you found it,
> Innocent virgin, let it remain.[79]

Circumscribed by words, unuttered at the center, such a truth retains the guiltlessness of silence. In both the final chapter and the discussion of Meister Eckhart, I shall suggest the possibility of a redemptiveness inherent in fallen language; we see some traces of this here. Words may be deficient, yet *once* we can live and say it, attentive. Into every gesture of despair Hölderlin's poetry of constant desire weaves a strand of hope; into every question of the future, a silent memory.

Rilke

Then the true poem is no longer the word that captures, the closed space of the telling word, but the breathing intimacy

whereby the poet consumes himself in order to augment space
and dissipates himself rhythmically: a pure inner burning around
nothing.

—Maurice Blanchot

The greatest gesture of despair before the effort to address the divine may be
Rainer Maria Rilke's; it is Rilke who supposes that he has no words which
could catch the attention of angels: "Who, if I cried out, would hear me
among the angels'/ hierarchies?"[80] At times, almost, there is hope, as if words
could, perhaps should, suffice to pull back to the world a God who is absent,
"extremely remote":

> . . . his emotion, which had grown accustomed to great distances,
> realized how extremely remote God was. There were nights when
> he thought he would be able to fling himself into space, toward
> God; hours full of disclosure when he felt strong enough to dive
> back to earth and pull it up with him on the tidal wave of his
> heart. He was like someone who hears a glorious language and
> feverishly decides to write poetry in it. Before long he would, to
> his dismay, find out how very difficult this language was. . . .[81]

This dismayingly difficult language is one to which he listens in unlikely
places, in which he nearly hears what even angels cannot. In it one attends
both to memory and to silence, to forgetting and to words. "It is not
enough," Rilke writes in the *Notebooks*, "to have memories. You must be able
to forget them when they are many, and you must have the immense
patience to wait until they return."[82] (Here, again, Bataille is echoed: meaning comes into its fullness only as forgotten.) Often, though, both parts of
the instruction are gratuitous; often we can neither remember nor forget;
often we have from the beginning refused to listen, or ceased when we began
to hear: "As if he listened. Silence, something distant . . . / We check ourselves and cease to hear it."[83] And small wonder; that for which Rilke
entreats us to listen may be the impossible.

> Listen, my heart, as only
> saints have listened: until the gigantic call lifted them
> off the ground; yet they kept on, impossibly,
> kneeling and didn't notice at all:
> so complete was their listening. Not that you could endure
> God's voice—far from it. But listen to the voice of the wind
> and the ceaseless message that forms itself out of silence.[84]

Here it seems that we are given the silence because the voice is unendurable; yet the silence itself forms in turn our fallen version of holy speaking. As Dianna Niebylski writes, "Silence, then, is seen . . . as the origin and final horizon of poetic language."[85]

Memory and words seek to preserve, yet fail. "We still remember," Rilke writes at the "Funeral monument of a young girl," "it is as if/ all this must once again exist."[86] But only as if; "all this" defies the imperative *must*, and our words prove inadequate to the space of our loss:

> I would like to fling my voice out like a cloth
> over the fragments of your death, and keep
> pulling at it until it is torn to pieces
> and all my words would have to walk around
> shivering, in the tatters of that voice;
> if lament were enough.[87]

If lament were enough; it is *as if* the lost must once again exist, if only we remember, if only we speak; it is *almost* enough, but never there. Our loss comes always before us:

> You who never arrived
> in my arms, Beloved, who were lost
> from the start,
> I don't even know what songs
> would please you.[88]

And so the silence which pervades our words may be a prior rupture; meaning may never arrive and may never have arrived. Certainly the destructive element that is death in Rilke's work performs the rending-open of time along with words:

> That we were frightened when you died . . . no rather:
> that your stern death broke in upon us, darkly
> wrenching the till-then from the ever-since . . .[89]

As it wrenches open time, so too death ruptures the meaning that words would gather over time:

> . . . strange
> to see meanings that clung together once, floating away
> in every direction. And being dead is hard work

and full of retrieval before one can gradually feel
a trace of eternity.—Though the living are wrong to believe
in the too-sharp distinctions which they themselves have created.[90]

We must be attentive to the last lines; our clear distinctions are too easy, and
to speak of loss is still too facile. Loss and joy turn around upon one another.
Death is one rupture of life, certainly. But poetry suggests that, just possibly,
we can wrap ourselves around this rupture, like words around silence,

> . . . this: that one can contain
> death, the whole of death, even before
> life has begun, can hold it to one's heart
> gently, and not refuse to go on living,
> is inexpressible.[91]

Here the silent, the inexpressible, is not simply death, but even its inherence
in life, or life's nonrefusal of both death and living, language's nonrefusal of
silence with sound. The inexpressible secret reverberates, nonetheless,
throughout our words.

And at the highest intensity of *life* the moment once more bursts forth
from time. It cuts though the length of temporality. Though death is "our
most intimate companion" to the speaker in the ninth Elegy, he continues
with the astonishment of the moment: "Look, I am living. On what? Neither
childhood nor future/ grows any smaller."[92] These astonishing instants are
moments of the purest attention, so close to the world in natural prayer that
we could *almost*; it is *as if*, we could name them to the Gods and angels, name
them and have them last.

> Perhaps we are *here* in order to say: house,
> bridge, fountain, gate, pitcher, fruit-tree, window—
> at most: column, tower. . . . But to *say* them, you must understand,
> oh to say them *more* intensely than the Things themselves
> ever dreamed of existing.

And then, insistently, "Praise this world to the angel . . ."[93]

We may have fallen, always already fallen; we may never be at home, but
always pulled away by a memory:

> the presence of what often overwhelms us: a memory, as if
> the element we keep pressing toward was once
> more intimate, more true, and our communion

infinitely tender. Here all is distance;
there it was breath. After that first home,
the second seems ambiguous,
and drafty.[94]

Ambiguity seems built into a language which is permeated by silence—by the distances between the words carried on the breath, by the breath which may always be turning back. Perhaps this second home is no home in the sense in which *home* suggests either origin or establishment, a place from which we come or in which we rest. Or perhaps *home* here has the sense Celan gives it; home "instead of all rest."[95] Yet it is the very restlessness, the fleeting quality, of earthly time which calls us in a later elegy:

But because *truly* being here is so much; because everything here
apparently needs us, this fleeting world, which in some strange way
keeps calling to us. Us, the most fleeting of all
. . . And we too, just once. And never again. But to have been
this once, completely, even if only once:
to have been at one with the earth, seems beyond undoing.[96]

At least one trait of this being, the context makes clear, is temporality; to be only before the immediate approach of not-being. And "never again" seems to intensify the momentary quality of the earthly, of the "fleeting world." It really is never again, in the sense in which even the return is never again, in which repetition is never pure, in which, as Klossowski shows us, forgetting is inherent. (If we did not forget, then of course the repetition, carrying the weight of remembrance, would not repeat the first instance.)

We are always on the edge of loss; we are always, says Rilke, "in the posture/ of someone going away."[97] Even if we are already lost, or at most ambiguously at home, our loss may already incorporate in some way our redemption. Our language wraps itself around silence; truly being-here, in this moment which is nothing but a purely arriving absence, is purely being nowhere; it is not *being* at all, any more than eternity is, but the attention to the passing which will enable memory. It is the moment which is not at all long, the moment so intensely attentive[98] as to rend time. Time is long: "but now you were in time, and time is long./ And time goes on, and time grows large. . . ."[99] Eternity is not long, and does not go on, and does not grow large. Perhaps we say to pin down, but truly listening we almost hear stillness (and it is impossible to say for how long, as we shall see when we read Augustine), something distant; we say something dismayingly difficult, we find in a fallen language the trace of language's own redemption.

To speak already of redemption is like speaking of loss: too facile. To begin to complicate our sense of redeeming language, we turn to a pair of religious thinkers, whose sense of time is as deeply curious as any we could find.

chapter four

*V*anishing presence: St. Augustine

open questions

What makes me shudder with love is not the heaven which you have promised me; horrible hell doesn't make me shudder . . . if there weren't a heaven I would love you and if there weren't a hell I would fear you.

—St. Teresa of Avila

Into this context of poetic allusiveness and elusiveness, of divine withdrawal and forgetful silences always just beneath language, St. Augustine of Hippo must come at first as a rather improbable intrusion.

We are most familiar with Augustine as a rather didactic bishop, dedicated certainly to rigorous theology but as much to the identification of heresies and, famously or infamously, to the vigorous repression of carnal sensuality.[1] But the marvel of Augustine, particularly in the *Confessions*, lies in the honesty of an intellect that doesn't turn away from the undesired or contradictory results of its thought. Undoubtedly Augustine would have preferred in this work to establish a securely self-evident, unchangeable eternity in which an equally certain God would certainly exist, but he does not halt the progress of a thought that opens onto a space from which time, presence, and meaning, even the divine itself, are absent or withdrawn. As Louis Mackey writes, "The problem raised by the *Confessions* is the problem of its own possibility. . . . The possibility of writing the *Confessions* is won or lost with the possibility of conversion and return."[2] That

Augustine allows these spaces to remain open may in turn tell us something more theologically and philosophically profound than we would have expected.

It is almost solely with the *Confessions* that I shall concern myself here. This remarkable text, one of the very earliest of autobiographies, is valuable precisely because it at times lacks the decisiveness of what may be more scholarly texts such as *City of God*. Instead it retains the honesty of interrogation; it holds open the space of questioning between human and divine. Mackey emphasizes the aspect of interrogation as desire: "The text of the *Confessions* records Augustine's attempt to transform autobiography (the language of necessity) into theology (the language of desire). His story begins in the forgetfulness of God and turns backward. . . ."[3]

Augustine's discussion of the puzzles of temporality is justly famous. Though Book XI of the *Confessions* is devoted to the exploration of time, Augustine has already begun his temporal inquiry in Book X. At first glance Book X appears almost straightforwardly Platonic in its evocation of memory [*memoria*], arguing that all we truly know is what we remember.[4] But the potential strangeness of Augustine's discussion, even for a Platonist, is apparent in the book's first lines; this passage on memory opens not with reminiscence but with hope, specifically a hope to know and be known by God, though hope is more customarily an evocation of the future.[5] This Book is less "theory," in a sense, than question and prayer.[6] Since, Platonically, knowledge itself inheres in memory, the links between memory and hope here are strong (as indeed they remain throughout Augustine's work).[7] Augustine acknowledges the existence of regret (hope's opposite and memory's more probable associate), but he regards it, interestingly, as an affective error, an inevitably misplaced longing.

Augustinian memory has an intriguing temporality. We customarily allot to memory only the past, but Augustine moves from the forward-looking hope-in-memory to the eternal presence of knowledge, that set of eternal truths which we remember rightly. He sees in memory a pledge of the future: memory draws him *forward*. As Denys Turner writes, "Augustine remembers God in the form of a restless dissatisfaction with all else that he seeks, a dissatisfaction which sharpens and intensifies as he draws ever nearer the goal of his seeking. That dissatisfaction is a 'remembering' because it is at once a longing for what he lacks and a recognition of the failure to reach it. . . ."[8] Ultimately, I would argue, memory is for Augustine a third thing beyond time or eternity, and in the end we find that for him, as much as for any later thinker we have read, neither time nor eternity nor memory will have been what we would have expected.

what then is time?

> My only labor is eternity itself.
> —Antonin Artaud

We shall have occasion to return for a more detailed look at the discussion of memory, but I would like first to turn to the questions of time proper. Augustine is prompted to his exploration of temporality by a troubling relation between the temporal and eternal: God, whose omniscience is eternal, can have no need of this confession which unfolds in time, a confession to which Augustine nonetheless feels himself compelled. Augustine struggles with the question of his own speaking—most temporal of processes—and writing, with his *need* to speak and to write.

Finally he concludes that the *Confessions* are justified as an overflow of his love of God. "I tell my story for love of your love," he writes; and later, "See the long story I have told to the best of my ability and will responds to your prior will."[9] Love turns out to be inextricable not only from the need to speak but from the ability to hear: "those whose ears are opened by love believe me," Augustine declares;[10] "The love which makes them good people tells them that I am not lying in confessing about myself, and the love in them believes me."[11] We must listen to know, and love enables our listening (as Augustine's "love of your love" suggests, it enables or draws forth speaking as well). The function of at once distancing and holding near, the *almost* of verbal space, echoes here. God's prior will to which Augustine responds links us in turn to the eternal Word, which can only be heard by those whose love, grounded in both memory and hope, enables them to listen. We recall with Mackey that desire, whether sacred or profane, is at the heart of the *Confessions*: "What is important for Augustine—the power that propelled him into language in the first place and, now that he looks back on it, the moving power in all language—is desire."[12]

So Augustine works his way into the puzzle of time by beginning with eternity, though one might think eternity the greater puzzle. He concludes that God must precede time as its cause, just as his prior will precedes Augustine's story-telling: "Since, therefore, you are the cause of all times. . . . You have made time itself."[13] God wills all creation, as he wills all speaking, including this story of Augustine's, from eternity, for all time. Augustine's take on God's precedence, of course, is ontological rather than temporal, avoiding the infinite regress that the latter would occasion. Having concluded, not too surprisingly, that time is God's creation, Augustine turns resolutely to the exploration of that created time itself. Both time and eternity quickly become vastly more complicated.

At first it seems that Augustine has set forth a successful and unexpectedly phenomenological theory of time, despite the confusion he avows in his famous declaration, "What then is time? Provided that no one asks me, I know. If I want to explain it to an inquirer, I do not know."[14] Asking just how we know or do not know time, he proceeds experientially and epistemologically: what are the modes of that knowing, he asks, and what is its source?

Time would seem to be most clearly known to us in the present. To know a thing is to be at least potentially aware of it *now*. (Here we might remind ourselves of that eternally present realm of true knowing which is Augustine's Platonic heritage.) But the effort to understand or define the present immediately faces a problem: the disappearance of that present by infinite contraction or division. The problem arises in connection with the epistemological issue of time's measure: how do we know, Augustine asks, how long a time is, or was, or will be? When is time present for us to measure, since surely we cannot measure what is not present? Trying to work out how much time must be present for measurement, Augustine considers smaller and smaller units of time. Having begun with the century, arriving finally at the hour, he muses,

> One hour is itself constituted of fugitive moments. Whatever part of it has flown away is past. What remains to it is future. If we can think of some bit of time which cannot be divided into even the smallest instantaneous moments, that alone is what we can call "present." And this time flies so quickly from future into past that it is an interval with no duration. If it has duration, it is divisible into past and future. But the present occupies no space.[15]

This is conspicuously problematic: ". . . we do measure time and cannot measure what has no being, and past and future have none. But how do we measure present time when it has no extension?"[16] In fact, the present seems to have as its only mode of existence that of an arriving absence:

> How can [past and future] "be" when the past is not now present and the future is not yet present? Yet if the present were always present, it would not pass into the past. . . . If then, in order to be time at all, the present is so made that it passes into the past, how can we say that this present also "is"? The cause of its being is that it will cease to be. So indeed we cannot truly say that time exists except in the sense that it tends toward nonexistence.[17]

To be, in time at least, is solely to tend toward nonbeing. Inexistence and existence become one another's temporal ground.

This passage already suggests that there is much more to the puzzle, since the present is only one of the three traditional modes of temporality. While the puzzle of presence lingers, we face others: if we perceive only in the present, how, Augustine asks, do we know past and future at all?

This is a question upon which Book X has already touched. There Augustine recounts the experience of speaking from memory: "As I speak, there are present images of everything I am speaking of, drawn out of the same treasure-house of memory. I would never say anything like that if these images were not present."[18] Something then seems to be made present when we remember, and in fact Augustine doubts the reality of neither past nor future events:

> Where did those who sang prophecies see these events if they do not yet exist? To see what has no existence is impossible. And those who narrate past history would surely not be telling a true story if they did not discern events by their souls' insight. If the past were nonexistent, it could not be discerned at all. Therefore, both past and future events exist.[19]

Even though the past is no longer and the future is not yet, past and future must exist. But the way in which they do so is, curiously enough, as modes of presence: "What is by now evident and clear," he says just a few sections later, "is that neither past nor future exists, and it is inexact language to speak of three times—past, present and future. Perhaps it would be exact to say: there are three times, a present of things past [memory], a present of things present [immediate awareness], and a present of thing to come [expectation]."[20] These modes of presence make it clear that his is an experiential rather than a metaphysical description: "In the soul there are these three aspects of time, and I do not see them anywhere else."[21]

This construction, surely remarkable for the fourth century, seems to settle the problem by making time into a variable of perception, perhaps even in proto-Kantian fashion a structure of the mind which measures it. But finally Augustine acknowledges that to measure time is as incomprehensible as to preserve it or keep it present: ". . . the times we measure are not those which do not yet exist, nor those which already have no existence, nor those which extend over no interval of time, nor those which reach no conclusions. So the times we measure are not future nor past nor those in the process of passing away."[22] Indeed, time's fugitive quality comes to seem more deeply ineffable than eternity's atemporality.

words in time

Trying to learn to use words, and every attempt
Is a wholly new start, and a different kind of failure
—T. S. Eliot

Still struggling with the observation that we do measure time, despite the
seeming impossibility of doing so, Augustine turns to a crucial image, one
that by now we will be expecting. For him the very measure of time is language, and language is as well the force of both divine creation and the creative outpouring of the *Confessions;* it is, at the very beginning, the Word.

"[D]o we use a shorter time," Augustine wonders, "to measure a longer
time . . . ? So we can be seen to use the length of a short syllable as a measure
when we say that a long syllable is twice its length."[23]Augustine reflects on
this verbal stretch in his suggestion that time might be "a distension . . . of
the mind itself."[24]

In this distended mind the word seems to be, in particular, spoken. Books
X and XI of the *Confessions* are astonishingly dense with aural metaphors.
Some are metaphors of speaking: the world cries out the glory of its creator;[25]
the narratives of memory speak their truth;[26] Augustine speaks to God[27] and
listens to him,[28] all in explicitly auditory images. It is even words which summon images from memory,[29] making them present to us.

It may be important to point out that Augustine makes note of our use
of *seeing* as a metaphor for all perception: "We do not say 'Hear how that
flashes,' or 'Smell how bright that is,' or 'Taste how that shines,' or 'Touch
how that gleams.' Of all these things we say 'see.' But we say not only 'See
how that light shines,' which only the eyes can perceive, but also 'See how
that sounds, see what smells, see what tastes, see how hard that is.'"[30] That he
so often uses the language of hearing instead suggests in this context a delib-
erate attention to both sound and speaking; these metaphors are not acci-
dentally or haphazardly aural. Perhaps it really is his intent to privilege the
auditory, the passing of language before God, or himself, or his subvoce
reader.[31] Perhaps he hears his words tending, not toward endurance on the
visual page, but toward an immeasurable series of slippings across the
thoughts of innumerable readers.

But sound and speaking are not the same, and they are most obviously
distinct in divine speech. In this speaking of God's, or between human and
God, Augustine discerns as well the silence we would think to be speaking's
opposite. Indeed, language whether human or divine hangs in the balance

between silence and sound. This tension is present from the earliest portions of Book X, in which Augustine is still wondering why he speaks to a God who, one might say, has already heard it. He confesses, he declares, "not . . . merely by physical words and sounds, but by words from my soul and a cry from my mind . . . therefore, my God my confession before you is made both in silence and not in silence. It is silent in that it is no audible sound, but in love it cries aloud."[32] Love, as we have already noted, turns out to work as an epistemological conduit for true speaking, a way of knowing it when we hear it, even if it can't be heard. Hearing draws out speaking, as silence—we have seen this already—opens the spaces so seductive to words.

In some sense we might argue that in temporal speaking, silence is overcome; it awaits the end in which the speaking will itself be lost. That is, there cannot be silence just when I am speaking. In the speech from eternity, however, silence is already gathered. Eternal speaking must gather silence because such speaking is full of meaning, and it is only in silence that meaning is found. That is, as Augustine himself will note, we understand only at the end of speaking. Language can re-sound in the silence of sound's absence, and indeed, as we soon realize, only in silence, where alone it has meaning.

In fact, Augustine recurs to the image of the speaking voice as a representative not merely of time but of truth, which, if he remains at all Platonic, is presumably unconstrained by temporality. "Concentrate," he urges himself, "on the point where truth is beginning to dawn. For example, a physical voice begins to sound. It sounds. It continues to sound, and then ceases. Silence has now come. . . ."[33] And in silence, we learn what the voice has meant. Meaning comes only after words, not in them.

God's Word and its silence, as I have suggested, present a particular problem. Augustine realizes that God may manifest a speech audible like human speech, as when the voice from the cloud declares, "This is my beloved son."[34] But the eternal, creative Word—the Word by which God makes world and time—is quite otherwise. "That word," Augustine says, "is spoken eternally, and by it all things are uttered eternally. . . . And so by the Word coeternal with you, you say all that you say in simultaneity and eternity, and whatever you say will come about does come about."[35]

In the passing words by which we measure time we find an unexpected recurrence to the human awareness of God and an unexpected opening onto the relation of human to the eternal divine. We are not measuring the time of the syllables at all, Augustine says, but, in the silence which finishes them, the memory of words: "something in my memory which stays. . . ."[36] We cannot hear silence nor measure time by it. But it is necessary as the space in which we know speaking; we can only have heard if we are to hear, to understand, or to know. In memory, not in time or eternity, we find the meaning of language, language between speaking and silence. In memory alone we find the measure of time. "Memory, then, "writes Denys Turner, "is the epistemological key."[37]

All we know or have of time is neither in the immediate awareness of presence nor in the past properly speaking, but in memory. Memory gathers what has been, whether temporal or eternal, what has just been or what has always been. We cannot understand a syllable or a moment of language in the speaking, but only a word which no longer sounds. Memory can gather only when the present has withdrawn, in the silence that follows or fills any speaking, following that which is spoken in time, pervading the eternal Word. It gathers what we know, what we remember, and even what we had forgotten: ". . . memory retains forgetfulness,"[38] Augustine rather provocatively declares, and ". . . in some way, though incomprehensible, I am certain that I remember forgetfulness itself."[39]

All truth, even divine truth, is memory. It is only in memory that we find the divine, the God who is one with the Word: "Surely my memory is where you dwell," Augustine says to God, "because I remember you there since first I learned of you, and I find you there when I think about you."[40] Augustinian memory, by virtue of Augustine's emphasis on silence, plays interestingly in and on the tension between Platonic memory, a stability to which one could always recur by proper attention, and a later understanding of memory as that which takes up what is over. Indeed, Augustine suggests that God came into his memory upon his learning of God; his notion then cannot be purely Platonic,[41] else God would only have been there already.

What is particularly astonishing here, in the claim that all we have of time is memory, is simply that Augustine has left us no time; his temporality is purely fugitive, and eternity, if it is the infinite mode of the present, can only magnify this slippage. It is as if we captured not a still point but the very fact of uncapturable flight. The interplay of speech and silence reinforces this sense: temporal silence holds meaning in the memory which follows speech, while eternal speech is already permeated with silence, is at no time spoken, but is already remembered.

It is here that we begin to understand why a chapter on memory opens with an evocation of hope. All that we have of time, and so all that we have of truth or meaning or God, is memory. Memory's "fields and vast palaces,"[42] are filled with what we have always known and already forgotten. It is all the presence we have, but like any presence it is not present at all. When, after all, do we remember? Not *now*; there is never enough space for a now; the present is at the opposite extreme of memory's vastness. Already, perhaps; perhaps we have already remembered and now remember that we had forgotten. Not yet, perhaps, but in the future to which we direct our hope. *I have the feeling that I'm going to have known.*

To proclaim this odd temporality of memory, its role in the always-vanishing, is not to deny the Platonic side of Augustinian memory, as that by which we come to the recognition of true propositions. "Astoundingly," says Augustine very much along the lines of the *Meno,* "when [these propositions] were formulated, how and why did I recognize them and say, 'yes that is true?' The answer must be that they were already in the memory. . . ."[43] Instead, the a/temporality that loops past into future reminds us that in this mode, all presence is suffused with absence, all being is having-been, even if it will be in having-been. All temporalities are swept into eternity's oneness, but it is a oneness of vanishing; and all meaningful speech opens onto the silence in which alone it can be both understood (it can have been heard) and lost, into the eternal silence of infinite spaces.

Time, for a proper Platonist, is like an inverse photograph, a moving image of an eternal stillness. But Augustine, in rendering presence impossible, has undone eternity with time. Eternity is the eternal now, and no 'now' can exist except as its own disappearance; it does not even exist-then-disappear. Eternity is not sempiternity, not infinite duration; it is in that sense a pure present without past or future. But every present is only the coming of an absence, an invitation to forget what has passed already into the realm of memory. Augustinian temporality thus comes startlingly close to the eternity of return, return playing memory to time's forgetfulness.

It comes as something of a surprise that Augustine does not resolve the puzzle of time or the question of eternity. He has available to him a number of exits. He could declare God's eternal being and his temporal creation to be beyond human comprehension; perhaps this could be intended to keep us humble about our intellectual capabilities. Or he might declare the temporal mysteries to be ineffable in being beyond language and understanding, yet accessible to inexplicable experience. In the face of reason's failure to cohere, Augustine could simply resort to faith, declaring his belief in the full divine and created presences that his reason seems to disprove, putting his faith in a higher authority despite if not because of its absurdity.

But he doesn't.

Augustine acknowledges his incomprehension, even after his best efforts to understand time and eternity. "You are my eternal Father, but I am scattered in times whose order I do not understand. The storms of incoherent events tear to pieces my thoughts, the inmost entrails of my soul. . . ."[44] Time becomes not a neat line nor even a circle but the very exemplar of fragmentation. Yet he retains a hope that, "purified and molten by the fires of [God's] love, [he will] flow together into [him]."[45] This desire, however, does not suffice for understanding. Augustine concludes Book XI by declaring to God, "you are unchangeably eternal, that is the truly eternal Creator of minds," while a person (in his own example someone singing, another strongly aural image) "suffers a distension or stretching in feeling and in sense perception from the expectation of future sounds and the memory of past sound."[46] Augustine appears curiously content with his impossible solution of regarding past and future as modes of the present, as if oblivious to the tension created in silence, in the disappearance of the present moment on which all time depends.

And this is odd in Augustine, who is oblivious to little, aside from the occasional Freudianism. He avoids setting forth the implication of his thought, but he has not avoided pursuing it to that implication. He retains perfectly the tension which even negative theology so often attempts to deny, refusing equally rational, dogmatic, or mystical resolution. His seeming abandonment of the problem may be quite as fruitful as the seeming abandon of a God who would forsake his son was to Christianity. Augustine seems to have forgotten the disappearance of presence and the silencing of speech. But we can trust that the text holds the remembrance of disappearance itself, that forgetfulness itself is bound up in memory, between time and eternity; in the Word, between silence and voice. Augustine is certain he remembers forgetfulness itself, and for love of what is silent and forgotten his words pour forth in time, in an appeal at once and indistinguishably to memory and to hope.

chapter five

$\mathcal{R}$edeeming language: Meister Eckhart

heretical questions

What is God? Why this question? Can God be said to be a thing? Since he is dead, do we not at least owe him respect for the person he was?

—Jean-Luc Nancy

In certain respects the pairing of fourteenth-century preacher Meister Eckhart with the fourth-century saint Augustine must appear as improbable as Augustine's presence at all initially did. Augustine, after all, has been canonized into the official communion of saints, and was, as I briefly noted, rather devoted to orthodoxy, to rooting out and condemning heretical doctrine.[1] Eckhart, in contrast, remains under condemnation for heresy (though it is a continuing project of the scholarly Eckhart society to have this seal of disapproval removed).[2] He himself vehemently protested this condemnation, of course. Certainly in some of his writing Eckhart seems no more heretical than any other mystic, a category in which he is often, if arguably, included.[3] Indeed, because his imagery and language are conspicuously noncarnal, he is less likely to shock us than any number of other writers whom he sometimes joins under the "mystic" label—writers from Angele de Foligno (with whose work Bataille was greatly taken) to Catherine of Siena (who kissed the sores of lepers, dreamt of drinking from the wounds of Christ, and envisioned being wed to him with his foreskin as wedding band) to Teresa of Avila (whose dream of spear-wielding angels reads today in inescapably Freudian terms) to John of the Cross (Teresa's

81

student and creator of highly erotic poetry regarding his relation to God)—
to name only a few of the most famous. The "shock" of Eckhart's work is
considerably more abstract.

It is arguable whether the propositions for which Eckhart was con-
demned (drawn from both commentaries and sermons) were propositions he
held in any heretical sense to be true. He himself claimed, "I can be in error,
but I cannot be a heretic, because the first belongs to the intellect, the second to the will."[4] In fact, it is not always easy to be certain of what Eckhart
is saying, and his own reassurances, such as, famously, "There is however no
need to understand this" in Sermon 52 (on the scripture "Blessed are the
poor"), are not always truly reassuring.

It may even be that Eckhart offended more by his manner of saying
than by his avowal of given doctrines. There are, among the sermons,
uniquely odd propositions and phrasings which seem almost designed for
the displeasure of ecclesiastical authorities: "Accordingly, if I say that 'God
is good,' this is not true. I am good, but God is not good! In fact, I would
rather say that I am better than God, for what is good can become better
and what is better can become the best."[5] While it is not altogether implau-
sible to see here a quite orthodox sense of God's unchangeable perfection,
there is something startling in the expression of the proposition. At the
same time, an unorthodox expression can alter our sense of what might be
otherwise standard claims; it is not always clear whether, still less where,
Eckhart really fits into the division between ortho- and heterodox. It is
somewhat more clear that these distinctions are not uppermost among his
concerns. Doctrine in general, in fact, is not his chief concern: "As with
other apophatic mystics," Michael Sells argues, "Eckhart is capable of a
deep mystical agnosticism."[6] He is as unorthodox within negative theology
as he is elsewhere.

Given this, the pairing with Augustine begins to make its own odd
sense. Eckhart's relation to Augustine's work is clearly respectful; he frequently and unironically (if sometimes rather loosely) cites Augustine as an
authority. Yet what is only, and at most reluctantly, implicit in Augustine—
the drawing of language into silence, a sense that silence and forgetting are
somehow inherent in our language (and this most particularly where that
language would relate us to God)—is, though with differences in particulars,
delightedly overt in Eckhart. In this discussion I would draw attention to
two of these particulars, which set Eckhart apart not only from Augustine
but from much of the negative and mystical theological tradition: the curious puzzle of the subject who speaks of God, and the interplay in this speaking of sin and redemption.

A digression into metaphysics is in order. John Caputo, in his excellent study of Derridean religiosity, *The Prayers and Tears of Jacques Derrida*, suggests that, "Everything in Eckhart is held safely in check within what Derrida would call, following Bataille, a 'restricted economy,' serving always to redound, to give back, *ad mejorem dei gloriam*, whatever is taken away, in a classic economy of sacrifice."[7] I too would give Eckhart a Bataillean (though not, not necessarily, a Derridean) reading, but with a somewhat different form. More precisely: with a sense that giving and taking away may indeed redound to the greater glory of God, but not quite with the neat resolution that this passage suggests: "As a hyperousiology, negative theology drops anchor, hits bottom, lodges itself securely in pure presence and the transcendental signified, every bit as much as any positive onto-theo-logy, and in a certain sense more so. . . . Far from providing a deconstruction of the metaphysics of presence, negative theology crowns the representations of metaphysics with the jewel of pure presence. . . ."[8]

But the "hyperousia" that Caputo attributes to negative theology, with Eckhart as its exemplar, need not be the sole reading of such theology—or perhaps Eckhart, like Derrida, is not a negative theologian. To more properly credit Caputo's reading, hyperousia, especially in a context in which Bataille has already been invoked, may be at the same time an intensification of being that ultimately negates its distinguishability from nothing. If Eckhartian negative theology resolves into the answer of hyper-presence, it is only and at the same time by dissolving into the question of hyper-absence.

In fact, it seems quite possible that for Eckhart, as for Bataille and Blanchot, the concern with the sacred is not fundamentally ontological, hence the possibility of a "mystical agnosticism." For Eckhart, from the perspectives of language and memory at least, nothing does not resolve into the being it bursts, nor silence into speaking, nor eternity into time. Nor vice versa in any of these cases; each instead marks the locus of a rupture, at once an inversion into an opposing term and a breaking of the opposition—a "negation" or inversion by intensity. And though my focus here, as before, is on language and time rather than on ontology or metaphysics, we find that for Eckhart language always bears the question of being: who speaks, and of what? Here the "subject" finds no Heideggerian dwelling in language, only the perpetual nomadic opening of interrogation. And to remember who is speaking, and of what, and when, is to remember the origin which he himself calls "a beginning without beginning."[9] To remember before the beginning means, for Eckhart, that we must also forget everything. And to speak of God means, even beyond the usual cautions of either mystical or negative theologies, to speak wrongly.

To some extent, of course, this too is familiar. The inability to speak properly of God is the universal problem of negative theology: how to say that the divine (whether entity or, in certain mystical strains, experience) cannot be said; how to justify saying that it cannot be said and teaching that it cannot be known. In this more customary line of negative theological thought (if the very idea of a customary negative theology isn't too oxymoronic) Eckhart writes that there are three reasons that those who have seen God cannot speak of it:

> Firstly, the goodness that they saw and recognized in God was so great and mysterious that their minds could not retain its image, for the images in their minds were all wholly unlike what they saw in God and were such a travesty of the truth that they preferred silence to lies. The second reason is that all they saw in God was so great and sublime that they could derive neither an image nor a form from it in order to speak of it. The third reason why they fell silent was that they looked into that hidden truth and saw there the mystery of God, without being able to put it into words. But occasionally it happened that they turned outside themselves and spoke, but then they lapsed into gross matter and wanted to teach us to know God through lowly creaturely things, since there was nothing that could adequately capture that truth.[10]

Here speaking becomes an act, it seems, of externalizing a truth, an act doomed to grossness and inaccuracy, but perhaps the only way of teaching. Amy Hollywood writes, "Eckhart maintains that the divine names show only the contours of what God is not, or at the most what God does."[11] Again, this puzzle is not entirely unfamiliar. But in Eckhart's version of theology, negative or not, there are the additional puzzles which will lead beyond any resolution into hyperousiology. It seems that logically, or perhaps ontologically (given the problematic nature of this 'I') or perhaps theologically (given the equally problematic status of this 'God'), I speak wrongly when I speak—and yet it is only by speaking wrongly, by saying falsely or saying what I have no right to say, that the truth can in any way emerge into a world from which it has withdrawn and which has withdrawn from it. And so to the puzzle of all negative theology—how to speak of a God who defies all naming—is added the puzzle of how to speak when I must be deprived of names together with God. I speak wrongly in speaking of God not only because God defies predication, but because in so doing, to speak truly, I must speak as nonself, and thus I cannot speak at all.[12] Neither, however, can I keep silence.

With this puzzle we are reminded of Blanchot once more. The "I speak," Foucault writes (precisely in writing of Blanchot), throws literature into question, makes it question itself by its very claim to the existence and action of a speaking subject.[13] But this phenomenon is not restricted to modernity, nor indeed to strictly literary language. Eckhart, as Bruce Milem points out, quite deliberately and quite often draws attention to the very fact of his speaking: his sermons are not infrequently, among innumerable other layers of meaning, discourses which draw attention to discourse.[14] Eckhart speaks of his speaking, of our speaking (that is, of human speaking), and of the very peculiar relation of that speaking to the divine. Again, for Eckhart, when I speak of God, I always, in some fashion, speak wrongly.

God as unnamable

> Or say that the end precedes the beginning,
> And the end and the beginning were always there
> Before the beginning and after the end. And all is always now.
> —T. S. Eliot

What we have primordially forgotten is, unsurprisingly, elusive. Eckhart nonetheless has something to tell us:

> When I existed in my first cause, I had no God and I was my own cause. I willed nothing and desired nothing. . . . What I desired, that was myself, and I was myself what I desired, and I was free both of God and of all things. But when I emerged by free choice and received my created being, I came into the possession of a God. . . .[15]

So in working through Eckhart, we find a remarkable challenge: it is not quite possible for us to begin at the beginning; the origin of our knowing and the ground of our ability to speak is the absence of origin. And not only of our knowing, but our wanting, our willing as well. And though Eckhart's sermons seem to be directed—insofar as they may legitimately be seen as directional or directive—toward a special sort of return, back toward this original everything/ nothing, it is equally plausible to see the mode of return as memory or as forgetting, to suggest that Eckhart wants us to hear the silence in his speech. There is no beginning except in speaking of it: "To start with, I understand from John's words, 'in the beginning,' a beginning without beginning. In God's name I continue."[16] In the beginning which is the Word, there is no beginning. In language we only continue, in the name of God, who turns out not to be a name in our languages at all. The divine 'I' is perhaps even more elusive than we would already anticipate. In the beginning, I am. "Scripture says, 'Before the created world, I am' (cf. Ecclus 24:14). It says: 'Before . . . I am,' which means that when we are raised above time into eternity, we perform a single work with God."[17] This "I" turns out not to function as we expect words to do; it is ambiguous between self and God. It is an indexical that no longer points. The 'I' who speaks of God is as elusive and mysterious as the God who says only, speaking of its self, *I am*.

This beginning without beginning—a sort of forgotten ante-origin—is also a peculiar sort of end without end. Perhaps Eckhart's sermons serve as reminders, recalling to us what we have necessarily forgotten—necessarily because this forgotten beginning without beginning comes only before us; *we*, as such, have never been there. Thus the peculiarity of seeing this beginning as also an end or aim, since if we aim at such a rejoinder we must aim beyond ourselves to where we, as such, never shall be. Hollywood writes, "Eckhart explicitly argues that there is no path to God. . . . For Eckhart, the act of breaking through into the circle of divine activity brings the soul into union with the divine and this very activity lies outside of time."[18]

The beginning without beginning, this anteorigin, an origin and an aim at once, sounds deeply odd yet bears more than a passing resemblance to, again, a quite traditional and in fact fairly orthodox idea in the history of philosophy and theology. Famous instances of nearly similar ideas include the prime mover of Aristotelian metaphysics—"an unmoved mover, being eternal, primary, and in act"[19] imparting motion to the universe "as do the desirable and intelligible."[20] The prime mover is the end of knowing and willing, source of all good and the "principle [on which] the heavens and nature depend."[21] Aristotle, in turn, influences Eckhart's near-contemporary, St. Thomas Aquinas, whose famous five causal arguments for the existence of God posit the latter as both uncaused first cause of all that exists and ultimate aim of the striving of every soul.[22] With each, Eckhart's thought shares a peculiar movement in which both creative outflow from and redemptive return to some primary or divine force occur, whether or not in the same moment, nonetheless along, we might say, the same path. Important distinctions, however, set Eckhart's theory apart from these. Not least is our sense that for neither Aristotle nor Aquinas is the human 'I' the cause of its own going-out from this "origin," nor even that it is contained within that origin. The Prime Mover and the Thomistic God have the power to create what is distinct from them, and this is not the same as emanations of that "contained" "within" them.

This image of emanation brings Eckhart closer to the cheerful Neoplatonism of Plotinus, whose One, emanating source of all, eludes descriptive language in a way that later negative theology will apply to God: "The One is all things and no one of them; the source of all things is not all things; and yet it is all things in a transcendental sense—all things, so to speak, having run back to it: or, more correctly, not all as yet are within it, though they will be."[23] And there is a distinctly Plotinian strain here, in what Michael Sells calls the "mystery" of Eckhart's texts: "Mystery is neither a set of abstruse doctrines to be taken on faith nor a secret prize for the initiated. Mystery is a referential openness onto the depths of a particular tradition. . . . The referential openness is fleeting. As Plotinus said, as soon as one thinks one has it, one has lost it. It is glimpsed only in the interstices of the text, in the tension between the saying and the unsaying."[24]

the I who speaks

In a sense, the "I" cannot be lost, because it does not belong to itself. It only is, therefore, as not its own, and therefore as always already lost.

—Maurice Blanchot

But Eckhart's language moves us toward a silence and forgetting stranger still than any of these. He is not merely Neoplatonic, but Christian; his is Plotinus by way of Augustine, and the ways of Augustine are strange. With the ambiguity of the "I" delivering these sermons, again, what is problematic is not only "speaking," as if it were pure process, but the very existence of this speaking "I". Eckhart seems, not infrequently, to speak *of* this I, seemingly *as* this I, yet as if the I were all, which of course is true of no "I". The first cause is only God insofar as God and I are not distinct. And so, of course, I am not I, nor is God God. To speak, even to speak of this nontime when "I" was in "my" first cause, is already to separate myself out from that first cause, to give myself the identity of one who speaks.

It is the speaking "I", the I who can say "I want, I will, I know" as much as "I am," who must fall silent, who must know nothing, who must, in forgetting, exceed every *must* in moving beyond and before any memory of itself. The speaking self speaks of itself, says "I," speaks itself, eludes itself, for if it is indeed at it own origin, it can say neither its original self nor, co-original with itself, its God. Eckhart has something to teach us, something we must know, but we must pass by way of this knowing and forget it: "But I am speaking of transformed knowledge, not ignorance that comes from lack of knowing; it is by knowing that we get to this unknowing. Then we know with divine knowing, then our ignorance is ennobled and adorned with supernatural knowledge. . . ."[25] God wants us to forget God, to get to unknowing, but in the highest form of unknowing we are not knowers to unknow. We, as selves and speakers, are not. *There is*, only, impersonally, a rejoicing in a wanting that fulfills itself. We are reminded of the murmuring neuter voice (voice of no self) in Blanchot, and of the joyful disaster that the loss of self can be.

Being, even hyperbeing, is not the true resolution of the appearance of nothing (unless, again, by this *hyper* we understand a Bataillean self-inverting term), yet neither is nothing the final answer. Eckhart, speaking, defies final terms, layers what seem to be contraries so that each becomes implicit in, and each requires, the other. And that further sense in which I speak always wrongly suggests, paradoxically, why I am right to do so. This sense takes in both the fall of language and its redemption.

fallen language

> Let these words answer
> For what is done, not to be done again.
> —T. S. Eliot

Although Eckhart does not show a particular obsession with the fallenness of language, nor indeed with fallenness, guilt, or sin in general, he does give us yet another sense in which a speaker speaks wrongly in using language of God: not merely because this is an onto-, theo-, or just plain logical error, but in a sense in which one *ought* not to speak, in which one errs in a sense much closer to that of sin. We must hear this cautiously; indeed, given Eckhart's customary optimism, we find sin somewhat secondary to redemption. (In this, too, Eckhart gives us a happier spin on a nonetheless Augustinian idea; for Augustine, sin, indeed evil more generally, is not a positive counterforce to goodness but simply the privation of it.)[26] Indeed, fallenness for Eckhart, the fall away from wanting what one is, the fall into words, may be a particularly Christian precondition of redemption, a happy fault. This "happy fault" is an ancient idea, and oddly enough one which lingers. "Taking it from the currently prevailing Sacramentary of the R[oman] C[atholic] Church, the text reads: 'O happy fault, O necessary sin of Adam/ Which gained for us so great a redeemer!'"[27] Redemption becomes consequent upon sin, grace upon fallenness. To be redeemed, it seems, is to remember to forget: to fall silent in the Word. The happy fault of speaking a fallen language is its ability to remind us of silence.

In Eckhart's sermonizing, temporality is explicitly linked both to mortality and to the impossibility of holy names. "God is God because there is nothing of the creature in him. He has never been named within time. Creatures, sin, and death belong to time."[28] Indeed, such naming, which must belong to time and hence properly to sin and death, becomes sinful itself when it endeavors to engage God: "Be silent therefore, and do not chatter about God, for by chattering about him, you tell lies and commit a sin. If you wish to be perfect and without sin, then do not prattle about God."[29] We cannot help noting, of course, that this imperative is itself given in words.

In fact, this is the only way in which it *can* be given; like any act, this commanding gesture belongs to time. Naming belongs to the world of action; that is, to separation from God: "The soul too is nameless. It is no more possible to find a name for the soul than it is to find one for God, even though weighty tomes have been written about this. But in so far as she chooses to act, we give her a name."[30] While it would be wrong to identify the soul with God, both share the character of namelessness in eternity; both are named only where fallen into separation, into time, in which they are distinct enough to acquire names. Holy names are deficient since what they name must already be at some remove from the perfection of divinity, but also simply because they are names at all.

Separation characterizes not only our distinction from God but also our distinction between silence and speech. God is "more silence than speech," says Eckhart, echoing Augustine once more: "The dwelling-place of the soul, which God is, is unnamed. I say, God is unspoken. But St. Augustine says that God is not unspoken; were he unspoken, even that would be speech, and he is more silence than speech."[31] Nor is Augustine the only authority cited for this claim: "We say that God is spirit. Not so. If God were really a spirit, he would be spoken. According to St. Gregory, we cannot rightly speak of God at all. Anything we say of him is bound to be a stammering."[32] Stammering is broken speech, and speaking of God, who is God because we are broken from him and can speak of him, is speech broken apart by, rather than divinely integrated with, silence. It is speech in time.

Yet like Augustine, Eckhart refers to the puzzle of a God who, though he ought not to be spoken, nonetheless speaks. God's speaking is creative, yet the time of its creativity in Eckhart's understanding is at least as strange as it was for Augustine: "God has only ever uttered one thing. His speech is single. In this one utterance, he speaks his Son forth, the Holy Spirit and all creatures, and yet there is only one utterance in God."[33] Though "the Holy Spirit and all creatures" are spoken for here, that one utterance becomes identified with the Son especially. In the world of time and separation, where God and soul are distinct, God-the-son speaks when the soul attains to silence: "If Jesus is to speak in the soul, then she must be alone and must herself be silent if she is to hear Jesus. . . . What does he say? He utters that which he is. What is he then? He is a word of the Father."[34] And indeed, "The Father has wholly uttered that same Word, as it is in itself: the Word and everything in the Word."[35] God is a self-speaking Word which utters everything. Yet this utterance speaking to the silent soul, properly rejoining word to silence (also rejoining soul and God, beyond and before the possibilities of temporal speech), overcomes the distinction between speaking and hearing essential to the very possibility of words in time.

To fall silent is not simply to refrain from speaking. Language is the bearer of meaning; what we know, we know in words. To "know" God, not in the fallen sense of the name but beyond names, is, in a term Bataille will later take up, to un-know: "We must sink into oblivion and ignorance. In this silence, this quiet, the Word is heard. There is no better method of approaching this Word than in silence, in quiet: we hear it and know it aright in unknowing. To one who knows nothing, it is clearly revealed."[36]

Our silence is essential to God's speaking, but it is only in the act of speaking and the receptivity of hearing that we can know this[37]—can almost remember that ante-origin—which means to pass by way of this knowledge, this memory, and forget it. Yet first we must remember, must have knowledge to transform. It is tempting for a moment to see a resolution into knowing as into being—forget what you think you know, and then you will get, as if in exchange, real knowing. But it is also "unknowing" to which we get; here too the terms refuse resolution. We must remember to forget: "Truly, you cannot be brought to know God divinely by any human science, nor by your own wisdom. To know God in God's way, your knowledge must change into outright unknowing, to a forgetting of yourself and every creature."[38] And there is, then, no more 'you' to know or to do the knowing.

This divine unknowing sustains rather than resolves. We forget and remember, know and do not know. We are not; we are neither distinct from nor one with God: "Where [God and the soul] are one, they are not identical, since identity requires distinction. And so I say that if the soul is to enter the divine unity, then she must leave behind the identity she has in the eternal image. . . . A pagan master says: the nothingness of God fills all things while his somethingness is nowhere. And so the soul cannot find God's some-thingness unless first she is reduced to nothingness . . ."[39]

But again, nothing does not simply precede and resolve into something. Becoming something was already a fall: "This is the second death and the sec-ond going-out, when the soul goes out from the being she has in her eternal image in order to seek the kingdom of God."[40] To become soul is to forget the unity which is no identity; it is to fall into separation. To remember unity is to forget self; to remember unity is to go beyond the possibilities of speaking, to be receptive to the word which names itself as silence. This is a receptiv-ity, though, to what is already "within" oneself: ". . . the Eternal Word is spo-ken internally in the heart of the soul, in the most interior and purest part, in the head of the soul, . . . in the *intellect*. That is where the birth takes place."[41] And so this birth or beginning of the Word, eternally occurring in the soul, and this pair of deaths, going out from and returning to God, become coextensive.

So too, likewise sustained, do desire and delight. Desire attaches both to the outgoing and to the return: "Then I desired myself and nothing else. What I desired, that was myself, and I was myself what I desired, and I was free both of God and of all things."[42] After this outgoing, that is, in the cre-ated world, desire directs itself toward dispossession—"for between God and detachment," writes Turner, "as Eckhart has said, lies nothing at all."[43] This is desire sustained by the very nature of God:

> There is no knowing what God is. We do know something—what God is not. This the discerning soul rejects. Intellect, meantime, finding no satisfaction in any mortal thing, is waiting, as matter awaits form. As matter is insatiable for form, so intel-lect is satisfied only with the essential, all-embracing truth. Only the truth will do, and this God keeps withdrawing from it, step by step, purposing to arouse its zeal and lure it on to seek and grasp the actual causeless good. God's desire is that the soul, not content with any mortal thing, may clamour more and more for the highest good of all.[44]

And so I desire(d) myself when I was indistinguishable from God; I desire my own outgoing; I desire a return but in order to return I must forget myself and God (and the desire that is mine), forget all causes. I will not attain this final satisfaction in God, for it is the annihilation of the distinction upon which "I" and "God" alike depend. I cannot forget until I remember my own first forgetfulness. We are not at home in the presence of all things; in the recesses of the soul, says Eckhart, "all things are present to you, subjectively alive and active in their zenith, in their prime. Why are you unaware of it? It is because you are not at home."[45] Nor can you be at home; at home, 'you' are not. At home there is only a self-fulfilling delight. Yet in the desire which pulls you across the space kept open by the withdrawal of God is another delight: "God delights in himself. In the delight in which God delights in himself, he delights also in all creatures. With the delight with which God delights in himself, with that delight he delights in all creatures—not as creatures but in creatures as God. In the delight in which God delights in himself, in that delight he delights in all things."[46] He wants what he is and he is what he wants.

Only memory will take us beyond us, before and beyond diversity. But memory here is indistinguishable from forgetting, as knowing from ignorance. This memory/forgetting as a movement of return manifests a double love, which overcomes its own doubleness. "You must love [God] as he is a non-God, a non-Spirit, a non-Person, a non-Image. Indeed, you must love him as he is One, pure, simple, and transparent, far from all duality. And we should sink eternally into this One, thus passing from something into nothing. So help us God. Amen."[47] And yet, of course, this "you" and "him," or speaking from another angle this "I" and "him," are properly indistinguished: "You should sink your 'being-you' into his 'being-him,' and your 'you' and his 'him' should become single 'me' so that with him you shall know in eternity his unbecome 'isness' and his unnamable nothingness."[48] There is nowhen and nowhere for this to take place: "God must become me and I must become God, so entirely that this 'he' and this 'I' become one 'is'. . . . But if thereby a single 'here' or 'now' enter in, then this 'I' can never become one in being and action with this 'he.'"[49]

Thus fully to approach God is also fully to retreat "into" oneself; to remember is to forget:

> I assert that it is more important for the soul to forsake God to
> attain perfection than it is for the soul to forsake creatures. . . .
> That we should forsake God is altogether what God intends, for
> as long as the soul has God, knows God, and is aware of God, she
> is far from God. This then is God's desire—that God should
> reduce himself to nothing in the soul so that that soul may lose
> herself. For the fact that God is called God comes from creatures.
> When the soul was a creature, she had a God, and then, as she lost
> her createdness, God remained for himself as he is. And this is the
> greatest honour that the soul can pay to God, to leave God to
> himself and to be free of him.[50]

We return by leaving. We must remember to forget, speak to remind ourselves that we must be silent; so that we can be receptive to hearing the name outside of fallen language, before time. When I speak, I have gotten it wrong, but this is a happy error. All speaking is fallen speaking, even God's. It is only in the fall of separation that God is God. There is nothing to know. There is no need to understand this. Beyond knowing, we are receptive to hearing a Word from which silence is never distinct.

chapter six

C onclusion: forgetful memory

And when without warning
the god stopped her and, with pain in his cry
spoke the words: He has turned around—,
she grasped nothing and said softly: Who?
　　　　　—Rainer Maria Rilke

Emmanuel Levinas, early in his work *Proper Names*, remarks upon and regrets the loss of eternal Platonic memory. He writes:

> The new anxiety, that of language cast adrift, seems to announce—without paraphrases . . . —the end of the world.
>
> Time no longer conveys its meaning in the simultaneity of sentences. Statements no longer succeed in putting things together. . . . It is as if Plato's anamensis, which for centuries maintained the unity of representation, were becoming amnesia—as if disorder did not necessarily re-establish a different order.[1]

Though my sense of language, drawn from the explorations I have undertaken here, shares this sense of drift, I would see in it no more anxiety than hope. I suspect that memory has been less replaced by amnesia than infiltrated by it, touched throughout by forgetting as the drifting language is by silence. And, as the readings of Augustine and Eckhart suggest, this anxiety is not wholly novel. Statements establish the order of things only in the service of a new disorder, with no order lastingly (re)established. Levinas, facing

an imperative he conceives as a moral absolute, seeking to preserve, turns to
names—indeed, to proper names, many now familiar to us, including those of
Celan, Blanchot, Jabès—and the name of God.

Leslie Hill, in *Extreme Contemporary*, points out this particular role of
the word *God*, remarking upon "the deep reservation expressed in *L'Entretien infini* by Blanchot about Levinas's persistent recourse in *Totalité et infini*
to the name of God."[2] Later, Hill notes, "As Blanchot and Levinas are both
aware, much here turns on the referent of the word God: species or genus of
supreme being, or proper name of that which is beyond being? The Christian God is traditionally seen as the former, while God in the Talmud,
according to Levinas, is unmistakably the latter; and it is generally the case
that the God Levinas invokes in his philosophical work is understood precisely not as (a) being at all, but as a name beyond being or nonbeing."[3] For
Blanchot too, the divine remains beyond being or non-being. But here,
where silence is given attention, *God* remains a word beyond naming. It is
not even the name of a transcendence which risks resolution into the opposite of human immanence.

This namelessness implies the absence of memory: what we cannot recall we cannot call by name. Levinas is right to turn to names in his efforts
against amnesia. The name, the name by which we call, must be vital to any
sense of memory; to remember is to re-call. To call by name evokes not only
the religious preoccupation with the name but all the workings of desire.
Calling by name evokes such intimacy that we are uneasy when others use
our names too readily, as salesmen often do. As I remarked in the introduction, silence is an erotic as much as a religious preoccupation; it is a preoccupation with the near but nonpresent, that which draws and is drawn, calls
and is called to. The one I call by name ought to be a friend; the name that
I call out is sure to be that of one I love.

Paradoxically, then, a preoccupation with silence calls to the name. That
is, it invokes the drawing-near of the ultimately, uncloseably proximate. Perhaps this is in some measure because ultimately, as so many of these thinkers
and writers remind us, at the highest level names are lacking. As Derrida writes,

> But to lose the name is not to attack it, to destroy it or wound it.
> On the contrary, to lose the name is quite simply to respect it: as
> name. That is to say, to pronounce it, which comes down to tra-
> versing it toward the other, the other whom it names and who
> bears it. To pronounce it without pronouncing it. To forget it by
> calling it, by recalling it (to oneself), which comes down to call-
> ing or recalling the other . . .[4]

Names, as Levinas suggests, are always needed; and yet they are lacking. Derrida adds, "And, as in every human or divine signature, there the name is necessary. Unless . . . the name be what effaces itself in front of what it names. Then 'the name is necessary' would mean that the name is lacking: it must be lacking, a name is necessary that is lacking."[5] Our words will always be wanting. Language is always desiring what language cannot have. To remember divinity or limit-experience, to recall where we never were, must be (as we have seen) to forget ourselves. And we, forgotten, will not be there to speak the name, nor even to call it out in ecstasy or sorrow.

But faced with the ungratifiable desire of language, we can only name, and we are right to do so. It is only thus that we can, like Augustine, remember forgetfulness itself, only thus that we recall the lack of names which opens up the space of silence. Amnesia in anamnesis, like so much else, had already emerged in the Augustinian obsession with his sense of finding or refinding God (centuries before Freud, he too seems to have understood this found object of desire as refound or remembered).[6] It emerges in that haunting claim of which Augustine himself cannot make sense, which he yet cannot dismiss, "I remember forgetfulness itself." Later, Meister Eckhart makes of this forgetfulness the very possibility of return. Yet this return to the desired means the loss of the speaking, and remembering, subject who might will it. Blanchot turns this haunting and haunted sense around toward an infinitely open future, repeating a sense of the future attained and lost: "I don't know, but I have the feeling I'm going to have known," while Bataille is in turn preoccupied with the reverse amnesia of the never-known. For modern and postmodern poetry, memory becomes subjunctive, an *as if*, an *almost*, never quite reaching past forgetfulness in the length of time. If loss and forgetting are primal and the original poem is withdrawn in silence, it is memory and desire which are all we have of time and of the eternal. It is silence that tells us where we never were.

Here we re-encounter the familiar apophatic frustration. In fallen words we undo the very silence, the spaces of which we would name, by speaking. It may even be the failure of holy names that preserves the openness of sacred space, the possibilities left by the absent god. We "name," we call to, a relation—to a space across which subjects may be drawn. Responding to Levinas, and to Levinas's recourse to the name of God, Blanchot writes, "Let us leave God to one side, the name is too imposing."[7] Too imposing, too strongly present, the name imposes itself rather than opening the space-between that proximity as well as distance demands. As Hölderlin remarks, "Near is/ and difficult to grasp, the God."[8] We call across the narrow distance but do not grasp the god and close the gap.

This perpetually proximate God might seem at the furthest remove from the always ever-knowing traditionally Judeo-Christian God, whose placeless place in our memories[9] is surely the reflection of our place in the eternally omniscient awareness. This god of forgetfulness is, surely, closer to the God of Isaac Luria, who creates by the act of his own disappearance, yet remains proximate enough to be recalled. The recollection, however, must always include "forgetfulness itself," and it cannot call the divine all the way back. And yet, as we have repeatedly seen, we find this absence oddly present in unexpected places. Forgetfulness, like this absence, ripples outward, tugging at the roots of memory. Blanchot writes,

> This will be the part of Isaac Luria. . . . One might think that the thought of exile . . . would definitely bring to a close the divine and earthly plans and deliver man to the powerless wait. But exile cannot be only a local event; . . . it is also the exile of God, the separation of one part of God from himself, the suffering of particles of light maintained captive in obscurity. One recognizes here the ancient conception of gnosis . . . it is Sophia, the light fallen into darkness, a being abandoned and yet divine, separated from its origin and yet not separated, for separation is called *time* and reunity, *eternity*. In most gnostic doctrines, it is through the sky alone that the divine soul, fallen to earth, can be recalled: there is only one possible action, that which is directed from above to below. However, notes Buber, in Jewish mystical thought, founded upon a relation of reciprocity, man remains the auxiliary of God. The spheres are separated so that man can bring them together. All creation and God himself lie in wait for man.[10]

But Blanchot's is a waiting, a lying-in-wait, without arrival. Both time and words move about in our nomadic exile. Perhaps names are lacking here too; perhaps we call "come" to those not suited by this wait, this injunction, this prayer—those we cannot call by name.[11] And perhaps this very lack, this openness beyond naming, this tear in time, is the ultimately generous understanding of a God without presence. This is not precisely Luria's God, because this generous withdrawal is prior to and indeed outside of any possibility of a union (re)attained. Still less is it precisely the Gnostic God, who leaves creation to a lesser divinity: this is creation by abandon; this is an a/theology for times more resolutely nonpoetic even than Hölderlin's.

Divine silence, not quite a memory, calls nonetheless to our calling, our language, the names we speak. Eckhart prays to that of which he would be rid, addresses his impossible prayer to—and for—the very absence of an addressee:

"Therefore I ask God to make me free of God. . . ."[12] And while Christ, fearing or finding himself abandoned, calls out to a relationality of divinity—"Eli, Eli," is rendered "deus meus," "my god,"—he does not name the recipient of his prayer, and indeed those who do hear a name in this prayer (a prayer, perhaps, to no one, calling to the terror of an infinite space) are mistaken: "He is calling to Elijah," the crowd declares, but he is not.[13] There are no names here, or there are failed names, names forgotten and forgetful. *Es fehlen heilige Namen.* We are returned to the lack of holy names. "Religious similes," declares the silence-loving Wittgenstein, "can be said to move on the edge of an abyss. . . . It would be different if at every turn it were said quite honestly: 'I am using this as a simile, but look: it doesn't fit here.' Then you wouldn't feel you were being cheated. . . ."[14] Religious language never has a truth to *present*, never quite fits in the places we think to have for it. It faces only an uncloseable open space, whereof, we must suspect, we cannot speak.

This divine space, this pure opening created by the absenting of the Name, opens language to literature as well (as Jabès points out, this withdrawal opens the space for the word). Levinas writes:

> The literary space into which Blanchot . . . leads us has nothing in common with the Heideggerian world that art renders inhabitable. Art, according to Blanchot, far from elucidating the world, exposes the desolate, lightless substratum underlying it, and restores to our sojourn its exotic essence—and to the wonders of our architecture, their function of makeshift desert shelters. Blanchot and Heidegger agree that art does not lead . . . to a world behind the world, an ideal world behind the real one. Art is light. Light from on high in Heidegger, making the world, founding place. In Blanchot it is a black light, a night coming from below— a light that undoes the world, leading it back to its origin, to the over and over again, the murmur, ceaseless lapping of waves, a 'deep past, ever long enough ago.'
>
> . . . Our concern here is not with going back in history. But for Blanchot, literature recalls the human essence of nomadism. Is nomadism not the source of a meaning, appearing in a light cast by no marble, but by the face of man?[15]

It is only the space opened by absence (including the silent absence of words) that allows us to be called: too-close proximity destroys speaking. But it is not only absence that calls us. Blanchot, for whom as for Bataille art is suffused with the sacrificiality of the sacred, writes of this in analyzing the relation demanded by artworks (including those of literature):

> This relation is one of distance. This distance is absolute. At this
> absolute distance, what appears before us, but as if without us, is the
> "surging forth of a presence"; presence is not something present;
> what is there, not approaching, not withdrawing, ignorant of all the
> games of the ungraspable, is there with the abrupt obviousness of
> presence, which refuses the gradual, the progressive, the slow
> advent, the insensible disappearance, and yet designates an infinite
> relation. Presence is the surging forth of the "separate presence": that
> which comes to us as incomparable, immobile in the suddenness of
> the coming, and offers itself as other, as is, in its strangeness.[16]

Here what presents itself to us is a strangeness so distant in its difference that it
must, at the same time it is present, elude us. Present and elusive, it evokes proximity: that which is near and difficult to reach. So we are led back once more,
called by no name to repeat again. "To be is to speak," says Levinas, interpreting
the words of Blanchot, "but in the absence of any interlocutor."[17] Or in the interrogation, the interlocution that every absence is, into the inviting silence.

forgetting to remember

> Begin to forget it. It will remember itself from every sides, with all
> gestures, in each our word. Today's truth, tomorrow's trend.
> Forget, remember!
> —James Joyce

Forgetfulness is primary to becoming, to returning, to language itself. We
must forget to speak, to write, to use words at all. "The point," says Jabès, "is
not to entrench ourselves behind the impossibility of writing and write only
of this immobility, but, on the contrary, to push to the point of impossibility
the illusion that writing is possible; for nothing is written that has not been
rewritten many times before."[18] To write and rewrite, we will have to play forgetfulness—both language's self-forgetfulness and that silence which language forgets—though memory. Only in this paradoxical play can we begin
to understand grace after the abandonment of the gods, and to invoke divinity after the failure of holy names.

    Memory, as Augustine tells us, holds meaning. Yet we see already that
such meaning gathers only in the silence of its own absence, an absence that
memory demands, though we understand remembering as its defiance. In the
approach of silence, memory shimmers with its own interwoven loss; eternity,
too, loses its static endurance and (in a tradition derived however indirectly

from Plotinus) becomes vibrant, alive. Eternity reflects a movement of delight and desire, of the natural prayer of attention, so intensified that the instant is taken outside the usual sense of moments passing into oblivion; it is affirmed forever and forever as passing—as loss and the coming of loss. It cuts through time, if we pay attention.

Memory and forgetting are no more opposites than are language and silence, eternity and time. They entangle in the murmur below speaking, in the present absence, the "strange lostness . . . palpably present." They are most entangled in the discourses of absence at its most profound, at the very edge of any possibility of meaning, on the other side of the threshold which is the constantly shifting border of language.

Thus the present's proximity (which never becomes the fullness of presence) returns to us in the Augustinian memory of the forgotten. Forgetfulness invokes absence as easily, and yet as falsely, as memory connotes presence. Levinas writes of forgetfulness in Blanchot, citing *Awaiting oblivion*, "She struggled, Blanchot says, 'against certain words that had been, as it were, deposited in her, and that she strove to keep connected with the future or with something that hadn't happened yet, though already present, though already past.' It is perhaps this movement—which undoes words, reducing them to the present—that Blanchot calls Waiting, Forgetting." Later Levinas adds: "Here, again, Forgetting restores diachrony to time. A diachrony with neither pretention nor retention. To await nothing and forget everything— the opposite of subjectivity—absence of any center. A relaxing of the *I*—of its tensing upon itself."[19] The "I" who speaks is fragmented before it finds or flows out into its identity. In forgetting it relaxes its tense hold upon the moment, and forgetting returns us to where it never was.

Nor, as must by now be evident, is waiting, forgetting a passive absent-mindedness. "Forgetfulness," writes Blanchot, "is a practice, the practice of writing that prophesies because it is enacted by the utter renunciation of everything: to announce is perhaps to renounce."[20] Klossowski, too, reminds us of the practice of forgetfulness—a practice, for him, essential to the active thought of recurrence, of eternity tangled in time.

eternity

It is the sun
Mixed with the sea.
        —Arthur Rimbaud

As time has its modes of past, present, and future—modes that become oddly disentanglable when, as Augustine suggests, anyone asks—so too eternity appears in at least two modes. The first of these, and the most obviously Nietzschean, is that of return. Here we may remind ourselves that the Schopenhauerian notion of return, grounded ambiguously in Western (particularly Stoic) and Eastern (he says Hindu) philosophy, is curiously compatible with time, at least in some of his presentations. Here, as I have suggested, it is not time that returns, but configurations and sequences of matter. (Once more: if time is infinitely extended and matter finite in quantity, then necessarily all configurations of matter return; necessarily, too, the order of these configurations eternally returns, even if we can scarcely imagine such a long time as this would require.) If we do insist upon wanting, valuing, remaining attached to life—contrary no doubt to Schopenhauer's hopes—then we ought, he says, to be reassured by this, as it guarantees the necessity of our existence. "If you could ever not be, you would not be now."

But Schopenhauer, as we remember, also suggests that we might more truly take an atemporal perspective. Time, he argues, is an imposition of human consciousness on an atemporal reality. It is only as consciousness that we worry about death, about change and ceasing to be. We impose before and after; we impose coming to be and passing away. Again, by implication, we should quit worrying about it.

This image of a True unchangingness, however, is less a notion of eternal return than of eternity beyond return. It is not unconventional, fitting rather into the idea of an eternal now, the *nunc stans* of Christian Platonic tradition. But the standing or staying of this 'now' is easily deceptive; we are tempted by the very words to read into it persistence and endurance. It is time, to be sure, that passes. But passage is also the very condition of duration: a long slow passage, or a sustained existence across a time which slides away beneath it. This implies that eternity does not pass, but that it is for precisely this reason that it does not endure. And so a less conventional reading suggests that it returns, and it fragments.

The Nietzschean return will begin as Schopenhauer's, but it will not be long before Nietzsche's experiential twist alters its meaning radically. The eternal recurrence in Nietzsche becomes not a cosmological construct but, as Klossowski says, "an *abrupt awakening*."[21] It is a thought, as we have seen Nietzsche argue, that will transform you radically or destroy you.

And, indeed, it may do both. This is Klossowski's insight, upon which Bataille and Blanchot both build. To think the "sudden thought" of return is to live in each moment an infinity of forgotten moments, forgotten selves. It is to affirm oneself as other than oneself, to affirm at every point a different choice and determination of the self; it is an infinite fragmentation of oneself as a series of possibilities. And the moment itself is fragmented with the individual who knows it, speaks it. It is transformed from a fixed point in a line of time to a point always different, always other than itself, a point we have always forgotten before we come to it.

Thus eternity as recurrence intercuts the second eternal mode, that of rupture, eternity as the cut through time. Eternity as perpetual return keeps time from ever beginning as an absolute original. Yet it keeps time always beginning, by starting over again without the option of completion or finality. Eternity as the intensified shattering moment of poets and priests slices vertically the horizontal extension of time, not to transcend time but to rupture it (as it is a moment on the line itself that intensifies). Here, too, time eludes us; it becomes its own outside. Joy and disaster coincide in the moment without duration and beyond accomplishment.

It still seems curious to entangle the vibrance of eternity, its intensity of life, with forgetting. Yet much as the force and beauty of language depend upon the silence caught up within yet eluding it, so too does eternity shimmer with its loss in time, and memory with the oblivion it awaits, where nothing awaits it. In Blanchot's narratives, writes Michel Foucault, space becomes "a long and narrow room, like a tunnel, in which approach and distance—the approach of forgetting, the distance of the wait—draw near to one another and unendingly move apart."[22] So Blanchot himself writes in Celui qui ne m'accompagnait pas, "Not speech, barely a murmur, barely a tremor, less than silence, less than the abyss of the void; the fullness of the void, something one cannot silence, occupying all of space, the uninterrupted, the incessant, a tremor and already a murmur, not a murmur but speech, and not just any speech, distinct speech, precise speech, within my reach."[23] This precise speech, though, this accessible speech, this pure eternal meaning represented in this crystal precision, derives indistinguishably from that murmur into which it collapses, the murmur under speech, in silence and less than silence, the too-much of speaking heaped up around a distinct and precise silence. In speech silence is already and again.

Eternity, as I quoted in the introduction, is something intensive about time. It is, we might say, time at an intensity of attention, of experience at the level of the inexperiencable, immemorial, of saying—more intensely than the Things themselves ever dreamed of (merely) existing. Correspondingly, silence is something intensive about language, language intensified in its communication, the secrets within language that break it apart.

forgetting

> As I am forgotten
> And would be forgotten, so I would forget
> Thus devoted, concentrated in purpose.
> —T. S. Eliot

Forgetfulness, as Jabès reminds us, invokes a pure silence, ". . . the silence that has forgotten."[24] Yet this purity of forgetfulness turns against itself too: "'Writing,' he said, 'is an act of silence directed against silence, the first positive act of death against death.'"[25]

What holds for speech, then, holds once more for writing as well. Our thinkers of writing are especially concerned not only with the order of things but with those disorderly events which can come to us only as memory: with madness and death, with joy and grace, with the well-remembered God of Jabès's "imaginary rabbi." Arkady Plotnisky notes that Bataille tries to make language remember what it forgets but also what cannot be remembered.[26] Writing, striving to make language remember what it cannot, is caught up in the peculiar time of return: "One cannot, I suppose, achieve the ultimate except in repetition. . . ."[27]

We have seen already how easily speaking evokes loss, how it slides toward being-forgotten. The silent voice is absent in a way in which the written word, the visuality of which is undeniable even where its impact is primarily though subvocally audible, cannot be. We listen to speech with a hunger founded in its impending loss; we speak, too, not only toward a future interrogation but out of the opening posed by the memory of the question. Blanchot writes in *Awaiting oblivion*, "What she says, the secrets that you collect and transcribe so as to give them their due, you must lead them gently, in spite of their attempt to seduce, toward the silence that you first drew out of them."[28] Writing does not preserve speaking; speaking does not preserve itself.

Speaking, more conspicuously than writing, demands as well the abyss of difference invoked by Bataille—the sense that speaker and listener can never quite come together. There is a generosity in speaking and listening, a giving of self which is, as much as in writing though without writing's detour through anonymity, a giving-up of self. In this double movement of language, this invitation to destruction inseparable from a delicately, precisely responsive attentiveness, is another doubleness. One gives oneself over to the return in a curious doubling of forgetfulness and mnemonic invocation. To love the moment, to say with Rilke to the angels,

house,
bridge, fountain, gate, pitcher, fruit-tree, window—
at most: column, tower. . . .[29]

is perhaps to perform what Eliot calls an "occupation for the saint," "appre-hend[ing] the intersection of the timeless with time."[30] To attend to the moment is to perform the natural prayer of the soul. To listen is to open space and to sustain this openness as possibility.

Forgetfulness unremembered would be time's triumph against eternity, a finality of loss. Memory unforgotten would overcome absence, making loss (past) into refinding (present), but after all, "if all time is eternally present/ All time is unredeemable."[31] Memory demands passage and absence. Thus it becomes not the restoration or preservation of presence but the call to, the invocation of, loss. Time is conquered in memory, but what is thus conquered is unredeemable time; it is presence conquered in time. It is only our own loss that saves us. Silence, I proposed in the introduction, presents a curious ele-ment of redemption; in the loss of time and language, we find too the mem-ory of the absent and the silence of speech.

Loss and exile, that is, become integral to salvation. We have seen already that the withdrawal of the divine may be read as the pure gift of exis-tence. Or language: the Word fallen silent to make room for words: "God withdrew from the world, not to settle man there, but the word." In the beginning is the Word: *in the beginning* means in absence, in divine with-drawal. Our words attempt to go beyond themselves but are silent at their center. They have their origin only in the absence of the origin, in the space without the beginning. When we forget silence, we have forgotten as well this exiled Word, forgotten that exile cannot be a local event.

We forget the Word, then, by forgetting silence. But that Word has aban-doned us with an inconceivable generosity; by forgetting us, it has made it pos-sible for us to remember. We cannot quite remember, though; we have only the sense of the search, of remembering forgetfulness itself, of the tug beyond self. "I well remember God." And when finally we remember "God," as Eck-hart reminds us, we are no longer present to perform the act of recollection.

toward a forgetful a/theology

Sin is the impossibility of forgetfulness.
—E. M. Cioran

Once again, we can return to Augustine to see memory and language not only interlinked but thought in connection with the divine. For Augustine, it is love, we recall, which both hears (which, in its listening, understands) and speaks. His confessions are made "from love of [God's] love,"[32] he declares, a declaration which provides some justification for his outpouring, an outpouring which is already an act of memory. Love is for love even at the human level: "This is what we love in friends," writes Augustine. "We love to the point that the human conscience feels guilty if we do not love the person who is loving us, and if that love is not returned. . . . Hence the mourning if a friend dies, the darkness of grief, and as sweetness is turned into bitterness the heart is flooded with tears. The lost life of those who die becomes the death of those still living."[33] A loved friend remains in memory[34]—in memory, with Augustine's beloved God, yet as the presence of death in life rather than as life everlasting. What we now suspect, of course, is the inseparability of these two: together they constitute memory.

We are reminded of a dual inescapability. We cannot escape from memory, but also, as Augustine's memory of his friend suggests, we cannot escape even in memory from death, as the inescapable detour, with forgetting. "Loss goes with writing. But a loss without any gift (a gift, that is, without reciprocation) is always liable to be a tranquilizing loss bringing security. That is why there is probably no amorous discourse, if not the language of love in its absence, 'lived' in loss, in decline—that is, in death."[35]

Literature, like death and like forgetting, is a detour, says Blanchot: "Discretion—reserve—is the place of literature. . . . He who speaks directly does not speak or speaks deceptively, thus consequently, without any direction save the loss of all straightforwardness. The correct relation to the world is the detour, and this detour is right only if it maintains itself, in the deviation and the distance, as the pure movement of its turning away."[36] We, as speakers and as writers too, are always in the posture of someone going away, always nomadic, always in exile.

We must, before we can return to eternity, take the unconditional detour once more.

This is a double detour which has been already and repeatedly taken. Plato already shows us this curiosity of memory; it depends not merely upon the infinite vitality of the soul, but upon death (though for him, to be sure, there is some conception of an afterlife). In the *Phaedrus*, it is only because we have fallen from the life of the heavens into mortal embodiment that we are tugged by memory, by the desire to return home beyond the body, meaning death in this world and removal to the world of pure spirit. The detour, as Blanchot has told us, is no option: "Forgetting, death: the unconditional detour." If the detour is unconditional, there are no straight paths, no memories reaching straight into a past neatly located behind us; memory always echoes with absence, circles through deaths, returns for the first time to the always-already-forgotten.

In the endless approach to recollection which is our exiled experience of the sacred, we remember without origin, return without finish. "Instead of finality, the burn of life which cannot burn out. From this fever all ending is excluded, all coming to a finish in a presence. Infinite, as unforeseen, foreboding. Forgetfulness, remembrance of the immemorial, without recollection."[37] Thus this memory comes to us not from, though perhaps as, eternity. It comes with a sense, naggingly vague or cuttingly precise, that we had somehow forgotten, and that here too forgetfulness awaits: "Oblivion, too," says Jabès, "is a pledge of the future."

And forgetting, as much as Augustinian memory, is a demand of love— forgetting, even beyond the specificity of absence invoked by memory. Roland Barthes, like Blanchot, sees love in language: "isn't the most sensitive point of . . . mourning the fact that I must lose a language—the amorous language? no more 'I love you's.'"[38] And he, too, finds here a language of absence: "This endured absence," he writes, "is nothing more or less than forgetfulness. I am, intermittently, unfaithful. This is the condition of my survival; for if I did not forget, I should die. The lover who doesn't forget sometimes dies of excess, exhaustion, and tension of memory. . . ."[39] Love's, however, is an impure and intermittent forgetfulness, not the loss of love itself: "I waken out of this forgetfulness very quickly. In great haste, I reconstitute a memory. . . ."[40]

As we saw earlier, Blanchot gestures back in time for the concept Roland Barthes calls the lover's anxiety, "the fear of a mourning which has already occurred, at the very origin. . . ."[41] Here I quote Blanchot at greater length:

> The Ancients had already sensed that *Lethe* is not merely the other side of Aletheia, its shadow, the negative force from which the knowledge that remembers would deliver us. *Lethe* is also the companion of Eros, the awakening proper to sleep, the distance from which one cannot take one's distance since it comes in all that moves away; a movement, therefore, without a trace, effacing itself in every trace, and nonetheless the expression must be used, however faultily, still announcing itself and already designating itself in the lack of writing that writing—this senseless game—remembers outside memory as its limit or its always prior illegitimacy.[42]

To forget, to entrust to forgetfulness (as we do in the generosity of speaking) is also to give ourselves more purely even than to memory. To devote ourselves beyond our individuation is an absorption beyond remembering.

Memory is always impure, and we meet in every direction a single point of silent forgetfulness, a point so close to the murmur of speech that in the end we no longer separate them and must return to begin again:

> There is only the fight to recover what has been lost
> And found and lost again and again: and now, under conditions
> That seem unpropitious. But perhaps neither gain nor loss.
> For us, there is only the trying. The rest is not our business.[43]

Indeed, the rest is not, at all; gain and loss do not come apart.

grace in exile: the happy fault of temporal language

> Redeem the time, redeem the dream
> The token of the word unheard, unspoken.
>
> Till the wind shake a thousand whispers from the yew.
>
> And after this our exile
>
> —T. S. Eliot

Forgetting intersects memory, silence, mourning, and hope. There is one more point of intersection we must re-mark: that of forgetting with the divine. Here, too, it must be language which calls us: "God speaks in oblivion," says Jabès, "His word means forgetting."[44] This divine oblivion is the speaking of silence. "God alone does not speak where He speaks; therefore God must be the silence where all words run dry. But then, if God is silence, what is this divine word we hear? If God is absence, what is this divine book on which we comment? And what is this human destiny that fuses with the silenced words of our books? No destiny for what has never seen the day. No future for what does not exist."[45]

Following Augustine following Plato, we more habitually set the sacred on the side of memory. For Augustine, though, memory must always remember forgetfulness too. We make the act of recollection for love of love—out of a desire that cannot attain to full satisfaction, because memory does not reach back in time to an origin but outside of time to forgetting. Lethe is also a sacred place, and oblivion may pledge eternity as well. Perhaps, says Jabès, our language is derivative from a divine silence, an effort not to respeak the word of God but to write for ourselves its silence, the "infinite silence" behind which our words always lag. Jabès, we recall, links this doubled silence to divine forgetting: "To say this silence means to say the sacred, but also, at the same time, to undo it." Indeed, the only way to say the sacred is to undo it.

In the sacred and the erotic—in language, therefore, at the extreme, at the edge of a final silence—remembering and forgetting become inseparable. Bataille writes:

> Forgetting of everything. Deep descent into the night of exis-
> tence. Infinite ignorant pleading, to drown oneself in anguish. To
> slip over the abyss and in the completed darkness experience the
> horror of it. To tremble, to despair, in the cold of solitude, in the
> eternal silence of man (foolishness of all sentences illusory
> answers for sentence, only the insane silence of night answers).
> The word God, to have used it in order to reach the depth of soli-
> tude, but to no longer know, hear his voice . . . God final word
> meaning that all words will fail further on . . .[46]

Jean-Luc Nancy writes, "There is the god who approaches man to the extent of touching him, and the god who retreats from man to the extent of abandoning him infinitely. The two are the same: the god who touches man touches him so as to leave him to himself, not so as to take hold of him and detain him."[47] In this absenting divine we hear the whisper of the silent word.

The silence at the center of every word echoes the silent Word, at once central and outside, rendering immanence and transcendence indistinguish-able. As silence empties out the center of every word, so too forgetfulness opens in memory, but memory opens onto forgetfulness in turn. Augustine suggests that forgetting is here incomplete: "When at least we remember our-selves to have forgotten, we have not totally forgotten. But if we have com-pletely forgotten, we cannot even search for what has been lost."[48] Jabès sees forgetting always within every memory, "Oblivion is the stillborn memory within all memory, which afflicts recall."[49]

Negative theology? Not precisely, especially if negative theology resolves into hyperousia, though the alliance is close. A silent word is a word still, a specific absence. To make better sense of this silent Word, of this forgetful remembering, it will be necessary to return to the outside of time, to the eter-nal. Eternity, however, is not far from time: "The outside is not the distant," says Levinas.[50] The two modes of the eternal intersect with time precisely as the outside of it: the instant of rupture with duration, the return of the same without identity. The instant intensified beyond the limits of the subject tears open time and saying, rips time from its trajectory to turn it back upon itself, forgets the orders of passage and endurance. To be sure, these may be instants of lacerating agony, of the emergence of death in life, of loss without the return of tranquil security. But to be caught up in the affirmation of the return, the disaster must emerge under other, joyful, names. It must emerge, in silence and as forgotten, in love and grace. Here is a more direct parallel with Gnosticism than that with which the absence of God presented us; Valentinian Gnosticism at least posits "the mystical, eternal silence" as the maternal principle of the divine, and as "the incomprehensible and indescribable Grace."[51]

Grace, of course, has long been both a mystery and a problem in Christian theology: that there could be this unmerited granting of God's goodness is clearly itself a confirmation of that goodness, but that this could be granted without merit leaves open disturbing possibilities. Grace's work is silent and somehow responsive; its "rules" are both immanent and inexplicit. We might see it as an invitation into a space, which invitation also opens the space for movement, a response which calls to calling. It is a joyful response to the invitation, which response invites the inviting. Denys Turner says of Augustine's *Confessions*, "It is . . . the story of the making of memory in a man who had lacked it. . . . That power which, from one point of view, he already possessed dormantly, needing only to be activated, from this other point of view is a new creation of grace, which opens up spaces in the soul previously lacking to it."[52] Grace will never be very far from memory.

There is a long tradition of opposition between the precisely worded law and the silent spirit of grace, one which we find already at work in the writings of John: "For the law was given through Moses; grace and truth come through Jesus Christ."[53] And Paul: "Law intruded into this process to multiply law-breaking. But where sin was thus multiplied, grace immeasurably exceeded it."[54] (And grace, displaying the character of silence, always exceeds immeasurably, while time is measured out by speaking.) Later Augustine, whose response to Pelagius, it has been noted, is largely a commentary on the letters of Paul,[55] makes much of this: "For they were under the law, not under grace, and therefore sin had dominion over them, from which a man is not freed by the law, but by grace."[56]

If grace is outside of law, it follows as well that there is no legislatable set of acts by which one can summon or bring about a state of grace. The list of such acts would have the force of law, transcendent, explicit, inviolable: if you do this, it must come. Grace as an open, silent space always entails chance and uncertainty. Paul, again, is emphatic: "But if it is by grace, then it does not rest on deeds done, or grace would cease to be grace."[57] And further: "For it is by his grace you are saved . . . *it is not your own doing*. It is God's gift, not a reward for work done."[58] Again Augustine echoes and emphasizes the point: "Grace . . . is not bestowed according to men's desserts; otherwise grace would no longer be grace."[59] Yet it seems clear that we can steel ourselves against grace—or can be so very loquacious that we drown out the very possibility of silence.

By grace or in grace we permit ourselves, however odd it may seem, to be unjustified and thus, as nearly as is possible for us, redeemed—but not as ourselves. The acting soul, says Eckhart, stays in time, while "the unity of the ground of the soul and of the divine is the basis for the work of the Son in the soul. Eckhart thus undermines the . . . scholastic distinction between originary and salvific grace. . . ."[60] It is by law that we die: without law, Paul seems to claim (the point is much debated) there is no sin; without sin (we recall our Old Testament) no death. It is by grace that there is life, only by grace that movement continues. But grace is possible only because of law, eternity because of time, redemption because of lapse, life because of mortality. The fault is a happy one.

Blanchot develops this connection in *The Step Not Beyond*: "The law kills. Death is always the horizon of the law: if you do this, you will die. It kills whoever does not observe it, and to observe it is already to die, to die to all possibilities."[61] Grace is the opening of spaces of possibility, an openness to the spaces of possibility which itself makes those spaces, a silence that draws language beyond the speaking. It is the transgression of the boundary keeping profane distinct from sacred, speech away from silence, time away from eternity. "Grace," Blanchot adds, "does not save from death, but it effaces the mortal condemnation in making of the *saltus mortalis*—the bound without discretion and without precaution—the careless motion (*la mouvement insouciant*) that concerns itself neither with condemnation nor with salvation, being the gift (*le don*) that has no weight, gift of lightness, gift always light."[62] The lightness of graceful motion is essential; it calls by opening space, not by imposing itself, not by demand. There is no one to whom we might bear this obligation. Jean-Luc Nancy writes, "Face to face, but without seeing each other from now on, the gods and men are abandoned to writing."[63] We owe only the generosity of readers, of interlocution.

breaking the law

> The law, without grace, would be impossible to respect, that is, to maintain, even at a distance.
>
> —Maurice Blanchot

In the beginning is the word, and the word is law. But law and word come to us already broken. There is more to be said of that break, of the moments of linguistic fall. Ours is a language always-already reread, re-inscribed, according to Old Testament sources. The Book of Exodus sets forth a surprising series of events. God speaks, first, to Moses, giving him the ten commandments: "And God spoke all these words," says our source.[64] But ordinary people, that is, everyone who is not Moses, have no wish to hear this fatal divine voice; they are more than willing to take Moses' words for it. Moses writes down these commandments,[65] but God decides to do better still. He calls Moses up to Mt. Sinai, where he is given "the two tablets of the Testimony, the tablets of stone inscribed by the finger of God. . . . The tablets were the work of God; the writing was the writing of God, engraved on the tablets."[66] *But no one reads them.* As soon as Moses returns among the people, he is enraged (they are not behaving well) and he smashes the tablets. He himself will rewrite these words at God's dictation: "So Moses chiseled out two stone tablets like the first ones. . . . Then the lord said, to Moses, 'Write down these words. . . .' . . . And he wrote on the tablets the words of covenant. . . ."[67] Others will neither hear God's voice nor read God's writing, but will hear and see only derivatively, only in time, only in the absence of the "original" voice, a voice inaccessible to the merely human ear. Divine words come to us, in time, already broken—as in eternity, already cut through (as Augustine has shown us) with silence.

The traditional placement of the fall of language comes still earlier, at the time of Babel, and is consequent upon human arrogance. "Now the whole world," we read in Genesis, "had one language and a common speech." And since the whole world is communicating so well, its inhabitants undertake the grand project of building a tower which will reach to heaven. This disturbs God: "The lord said, 'If as one people speaking the same language they have begun to do this, then nothing they plan to do will be impossible for them. Come, let us go down and confuse their language so they will not understand each other.'"[68] Babel, the loss of innocence in speaking, "both replicates and internalizes the exile from Eden," writes Marianne Shapiro: "After the first sin God withdrew from man. When he separated man from Himself at Babel, the confusion of tongues founded initially on a growing number of languages became a sign for the whole sinful city."[69] Here is indeed a replication, the withdrawal of god and the withdrawal of meaning, or at any rate the intelligibility and communicability of meaning across peoples. There is a multiplicity within languages too, a multiplicity which suggests not a set of private languages but a series of interrogative openings. But to speak of loss, of innocence or meaning or god, is still too facile. In loss is the very possibility of the joy of redemption; through postlapsarian language runs the underlying, silent, and impersonal almost-murmur of grace.

In language itself, in the multiplicity inherent in any language, in the uncloseable distance across speakers, listeners, readers, writers—in the otherness that poetry most explicitly brings into play—there is already, again, some redemptive mode. Language is not only the place of the multiple fall, but the first and most joyous gift, as Dante suggests in *De vulgari eloquentia*: ". . . the first word," writes Marianne Shapiro in her elegant reading of this text, "must have been *God*, 'El'—" she quotes Dante: "for it is absurd and repugnant to reason that anything could have been named by man before God, by whom and for whom he had been created. . . . [I]t stands to reason that he . . . began his utterance with joy; and since there is no joy outside God, and God Himself is all joy, it follows that the first speaker first of all spoke the word 'God.'"[70]

On this perspective, then, the first gift is the name itself—a name which is withdrawn well before Babel in the God who is unnamed, who will say of itself only, "I am." Yet there is language yet, even if it has fallen it is words still. There is, then, grace as well as confusion in our words; there is that impossible "original" poem—an original rupture, a grace already enwrapt in its guilt, a silence accessible to us only when we have heaped our words around it, too much—only in too little time, a moment burst beyond any time at all. The invocation of silence is the creation of the otherness of language. It is interrogation and hence opens onto the future. It gestures beyond the end as well as before the origin; it opens the space of address but demands no answer. "I make no demands here," and here are no angels to hear us. The question is neither enough nor little enough; it is excess and deficiency; it too is rupture, and after the end we are back before the beginning.

This is a redemption outside transcendence, yet not precisely immanent either; it is the redemption inherent in exile. As Leslie Hill writes, "Blanchot's prognosis differs crucially from that of Heidegger. While for Heidegger it was an article of conviction, as he puts it in his posthumous *Spiegel* interview, that 'only a god can still save us', for Blanchot the time of distress is not a time of salvation or nostalgia for salvation, but the time of art, the time of the absence of time."[71] The absence of time (where the genetive takes a double sense, evoking passage and loss) is not only distancing but seductive; not only disaster but that which comes to us under the other, joyful name of grace.

The law comes to us broken, yet as if it were the first; it comes to us as the first law we have, without original. The first Word is likewise lost; we have only its repetition, a copy by which we remember forgetfulness itself, remember what we have never seen, remember *that* we have never seen. At its very arrival we know that we can also forget the Law, that it can be broken, even if and even though, by definition, we must not break the Law. But like silence, it cannot be kept. We are not alone in being able to break the Law: it, too, may be suspended in silence, by grace, beyond time. In its very fall, in falling silent, the word redeems the time.

E ndnotes

In a work dealing with language, it seems to me there is some value in reproducing cited words in the languages in which they were written. I have not done so for texts of which I have made only minor use nor for some works I have been unable to track down (this is especially true for chapter five). In general, however, I have attempted to supply original-language citations as well as those to the translations I have used.

introduction

1. Immanuel Kant, *Critique of pure reason*, 1781, translated by Norman Kemp Smith (NY: St. Martin's Press, 1965), 35, 35n.

2. Ludwig Wittgenstein, *Tractatus logico-philosophicus*, bilingual edition, translated by C. K. Ogden (London: Routledge and Kegan Paul, 1922) point 7.

"Wovon man nicht sprechen kann, darüber muß man schweigen." *Logisch-philosophisch Abhandlung*, 7, in same edition.

3. Michael Sells, *Mystical languages of unsaying* (Chicago: University of Chicago Press, 1994), 4.

4. Louis Mackey, *Peregrinations of the Word: Essays in medieval philosophy* (Ann Arbor: University of Michigan Press, 1997), 9.

5. Jean Baudrillard, *Seduction*, translated by Brian Singer (NY: St. Martin's Press, 1990), 1.

"L'ère bourgeoise est vouée à la nature et à la production . . ." *De la séduction* (Paris: Éditions Galilée, 1979), 9.

6. Georges Bataille, *Erotism*, translated by Mary Dalwood (San Francisco: City Lights Press, 1986), 264.

". . . l'érotism était silence, . . . il était solitude. Mais il ne l'est pas pour ceux dont la présence au monde, à elle seule, est pure négation du silence, bavardage, oubli de la solitude possible." *L'Érotisme* (Paris: Éditions de Minuit, 1957), 289.

7. *Seduction*, 20.

". . . dans une culture qui produit tout, qui fait tout parler, tout jouir, tout discourir." *Séduction*, 35.

8. T. S. Eliot, "Burnt Norton," in *Four Quartets* (New York: Harcourt Brace Jovanovich, 1943).

9. Georges Bataille, *Inner experience*, translated by Leslie Anne Boldt (Albany: SUNY Press, 1988), 16. Hereafter IE.

"Je ne donnerai qu'un exemple de *mot* glissant. Je dis *mot*: ce peut être aussi bien la phrase où l'on insère le mot, mais je me borne au mot *silence*. Du mot il es déjà . . . l'abolition du bruit qu'est le mot; entre tous le mots c'est le plus pervers, ou le plus poétique: il est lui-même gage de sa mort." *L'expérience intérieure* (Paris: Gallimard, 1954), 28. Hereafter, L'EI.

10. Denys Turner, *The darkness of God: Negativity in Christian mysticism* (Cambridge, UK: Cambridge University Press, 1995), 150.

11. Emmanuel Levinas, *Proper names*, translated by Michael B. Smith (Stanford: Stanford University Press, 1996), 127. Hereafter, PN.

"Blanchot ne voit pas dans la philosophie l'ultime possibilité, ni, d'ailleurs, dans la possibilité l'humain. Ce siècle aura done été pour tous la fin de la philosophie! Pour ceux qui veulent bâtir un monde meilleur—changer et non seulement comprendre. Pour ceux qui, à leurs antipodes, remontent avec Heidegger à la «vérité de l'être» . . . La pensée contemporaine nous réserve la surprise d'un athéisme qui n'est pas humaniste: les dieux sont morts ou retirés du monde; l'homme concret, même raisonnable ne contient pas l'univers." *Sur Maurice Blanchot* (Paris: Fata Morgana, 1975), 9–10. Hereafter, SMB.

12. Anselm, *Proslogion*, translated by M. J. Charlesworth (Notre Dame: University of Notre Dame Press, 1979), chapter XIX.

"Non ergo fuisti heri aut eris cras, sed heri et hodie et cras es." In the same edition.

13. Edmond Jabès, *The book of resemblances*, volume 3: *The Ineffaceable, the Unperceived*, translated by Rosmarie Waldrop (Hanover, NH: Wesleyan University Press, 1991), 51. Italics and ellipsis original. Hereafter, TBR.

"*Pour vous, hier et demain sont courbes du même cercle infernal et vos bonds d'outre-clôture, tant de plaies dans leur mal. . . .*" *Le livre des ressemblances*, (Paris: Gallimard, 1980), 342. Hereafter, LR.

14. See Friedrich Nietzsche, *The Will to power*, translated by Walter Kaufmann and R. J. Hollingdale (NY: Vintage Books, 1968), sections 481–490. Hereafter, WP.

15. Although not every author maintains this distinction, it is an important one. *Sempiternity* is the infinite duration of time, stretching before and after any given moment. *Eternity*, however, is properly outside of time, in an odd and more conceptually difficult relation to any given temporal moment.

16. "Nocturnally pouting" in Paul Celan, *Poems of Paul Celan*, translated by Michael Hamburger, bilingual edition (NY: Persea Books, 1988), 91.

"Ein Wort—du weißt:/ eine Leiche." "Nächtlich Geschürzt," 90. Hereafter, PPC.

17. Jabès, TBR, vol. 3, 32.

"Toute silence rompt un silence originel contre lequel elle luttera jusqu'à la mort. L'éternité serait, peut-être, ce temps muet, infini en eval du temps." LR, 321.

18. Friedrich Nietzsche, *The Gay Science*, translated by Walter Kaufmann, NY: Vintage, 1974. Hereafter, GS.

"Wie, wenn dir eines Tages oder Nachts ein Dämon in deine einsamste Einsamkeit nachschliche und dir sagte: »Dieses Leben, wie du es jetzt lebst und gelebt hast, wirst du noch einmal und noch unzählige Male leben müßen; und es wird nichts Neues daran sein, sondern jeder Schmerz und jede Lust und jeder Gedanke und Seufzer und alles unsäglich Kleine und Große deines Lebens muß dir wiederkommen, und alles in derselben Reihe und Folge— . . . —Würdest du dich nicht niederwerfen und mit den Zähnen knirschen und den Dämon verfluchen, der so redete? Oder hast du einmal einen ungeheuren Augenblick erlebt, wo du ihm antworten würdest: »du bist ein Gott und nie hörte ich Göttlicheres!«" *Die Fröliche Wissenschaft*, in *Werke II* (Frankfurt: Ullstein, 1984), section 341. Hereafter, FW.

19. See "On death and its relation to the indestructibility of our true nature," in *The will to live: selected writings of Arthur Schopenhauer*, edited by Richard Taylor (NY: Anchor Books, 1962), 132.

20. In this Schopenhauer goes beyond the Kantian metaphysics he professes to endorse. Kant himself claims that we cannot know whether things in themselves are identical with or even resemble our perception of them. Like Schopenhauer, he acknowledges that they may not be; unlike Schopenhauer, he also grants that they may. Schopenhauer, ibid., 131f. Kant, op.cit., "Summary representation of the correctness of this deduction of the pure concepts of the understanding . . ." A128–29, 149–50.

21. Michel Haar, "Nietzsche and philosophical language," in *The new Nietzsche*, edited by David Allison (Cambridge: MIT Press, 1977), 6.

22. Pierre Klossowski, "The experience of the eternal return," in *Nietzsche and the vicious circle*, translated by Daniel W. Smith (Chicago: University of Chicago Press, 1997), 57. Hereafter, NVC.

"*L'anamnèse* coïncide avec la révélation du Retour: Comment le Retour ne ramène-t-il pas l'oubli? Non seulement j'apprends que moi (Nietzsche) je me trouve revenu à l'instant crucial où culmine l'éternité du cercle, alors même que la vérité du retour nécessaire m'est révélée; mais j'apprends du même coup que j'étais *autre* que je ne le suis *maintenant*, pour l'avoir oubliée, donc que je suis devenu un autre en l'apprenant; vais-e changer et oublier une fois de plus que je changerai nécessairement pendant une éternité—jusqu'à ce que je réapprenne à nouveau cette révélation?" *Nietzsche et le cercle vicieux* (Paris: Mercure de France, 1975), 94. Hereafter, NCV.

23. Maurice Blanchot, *The step not beyond*, translated by Lycette Nelson (Albany: SUNY Press, 1992), 11. Hereafter, SNB.

". . . la loi du retour, valant pour, tout le passé et pour tout l'avenir, ne te permettra jamais, sauf par un malentendu, de te laisser une place dans un présent possible, ni de laisser nulle présence venir jusqu'à toi." *Le pas au delà* (Paris: Gallimard, 1973), 20. Hereafter, PAD.

24. ". . . whoever sees, even only in general, that his existence rests upon some kind of original necessity will not believe that this which has produced so wonderful a thing is limited to such a brief span of time, but that it is active in every one. But he will recognize his existence as necessary who reflects that up till now, when he exists, already an infinite time, thus also an infinity of changes, has run its course, but in spite of this he yet exists; thus the whole range of all possible states has already exhausted itself without being able to destroy his existence. *If he could ever not be, he would already not be now. . . . what exists, exists necessarily.*" Arthur Schopenhauer, "On the Assertion of the Will to Live," chapter xlv from Supplements to the fourth book of *The World as Will and Idea,* in *The Will to Live,* 145.

25. Leslie Hill, *Maurice Blanchot: Extreme Contemporary* (NY: Routledge, 1997), 193. Hereafter, MBEC.

26. Peter Manchester, "The Religious Experience of Time and Eternity," in *Classical Mediterranean Spirituality,* edited by A. H. Armstrong (NY: Crossroads, 1986), 384.

27. Ibid., 398.

28. Rainer Maria Rilke, "An die Musik," in *Sammtliche Werke* , II, 111. Cited and translated by Dianna C. Niebylski, *The poem on the edge of the world: the limits of language and the uses of silence in the poetry of Malarmé, Rilke, and Vallejo* (NY: Peter Lang, 1993).

". . . Du Sprache wo Sprachen /enden. Du Zeit,/ die senkrecht steht auf der Richtung vergehender Herzen." ibid.

29. "you remain, you remain/ a dead woman's child, / to the No of my longing consecrated/ wedded to a fissure in time /to which I was led by a mother's word. . . ." "In front of a candle," PPC, 87.

"Du bleibst, du bleibst, du bleibst/ einer Toten Kind,/ geweiht dem Nein meiner Sehnsucht,/ vermählt einer Schrunde der Zeit,/ vor die mich das Mutterwort führte . . ." "Vor einer Kerze," PPC, 86.

30. "Letter on Humanism," in *Martin Heidegger: Basic writings,* edited by David Farrell Krell (NY: Harper and Row, 1977), 230. Hereafter, MHBW.

"Wie soll denn der Mensch der gegenwärtigen Weltgeschichte auch nur ernst und streng fragen können, ob der Gott sich nahe oder entziehe . . ." "Brief über den »Humanismus«," *Wegmarken* (Frankfurt: Vittorio Klostermann, 1967), 182. Hereafter, BUH.

31. "Letter on Humanism," MHBW, 199.

"Die Sprache . . . das Haus der Wahrheit des Seins ist." BUH, 150.

32. MHBW, 193.

"In ihrer Behausung wohnt der Mensch." BUH, 145.

33. See "What calls for thinking?" in MHBW, 358.

"Was heisst Denken?" (Tübingen: Max Niemeyer Verlag, 1971), 50–51. Hereafter, WHD.

34. "What calls for thinking?," MHBW, 348–50. WHD, 3–6.

35. "What calls for thinking?" 345.

". . . wir mögen wiederum wahrhaft nur Jenes, was seinerseits uns selber und zwar uns in unserem Wesen mag, indem es sich unserem Wesen als das zuspricht, was uns im Wesen hält. Halten heißt eigentlich hüten. . . . Was uns in unserem Wesen hält, hält uns jedoch nur so lange, als wir selber von uns her das Haltende be-halten. Wir be-halten es, wenn wir es nicht aus dem Gedächtnis lassen." WHD, 1.

36. See "On the essence of truth," MHBW 117–41.

Wegmarken, 73–97.

37. "Letter on humanism," MHBW, 203.

"Die Metaphysik fragt nicht nach der Wahrheit des Seins selbst. Sie fragt daher auch nie, in welcher Weise das Wesen des Menschen zur Wahrheit des Seins gehört." BUH, 154.

38. See "What calls for thinking," MHBW 364–66.

WHD, 82–85.

39. Gershom Scholem, Major trends in Jewish mysticism (NY: Schocken Books, 1971), 12, cited in Richard Stamelman, "Nomadic writing: the poetics of exile," in Edmond Jabès: The sin of the book, edited by Eric Gould (Lincoln: University of Nebraska Press, 1985), 102. Hereafter, EJSB. Shaul Magid points out the existence of a similar idea in the Hasidic thought of Rabbi Nahman. See Shaul Magid, "Through the void: the absence of God in R. Nahman of Bratzlav's Likkutei MoHaRan," Harvard theological review, 88 (October 1995), 495–519.

40. David Biale, "Jewish mysticism in the sixteenth century," in Medieval Mystics, edited by Paul Szarmach (Albany: SUNY Press, 1984), 322. Hereafter, JMSC.

41. Ibid., 325.

42. Gershom Scholem, The Messianic idea in Judaism and other essays on Jewish spirituality (NY: Schocken Books, 1971), 45, cited in Stamelman, EJSB, 103.

43. Mircea Eliade, The sacred and the profane: the nature of religion, translated by Willard R. Trask (NY: Harcourt Brace Jovanovich, 1959), 121–22. I am grateful to Peter Manchester for pointing out this passage to me. I am indebted to him as well for other references and helpful reminders throughout the discussion of the absent god.

44. David Biale, Gershom Scholem: Kabbalah and Counter-History, (Cambridge: Harvard University Press, second edition 1982), 52. Hereafter, GSKC.

45. Ibid., 81.

46. Biale, JMSC, 323.

47. Ibid.

48. Biale, GSKC, 60.

49. Hill, MBEC, 161.

chapter one

1. "Thanks (be given) to Jacques Derrida," in *The Blanchot reader*, edited by Michael Holland (Oxford: Blackwell, 1995), translated by Leslie Hill, 317.

2. Maurice Blanchot, *The writing of the disaster*, translated by Ann Smock (Lincoln: University of Nebraska Press, 1986), 99. Hereafter, WD.

"ni lire, ni écrire, ni parler . . ." *L'écriture du Désastre* (Paris: Gallimard, 1980) , 154. Hereafter, ED.

3. A common classicatory scheme for Blanchot's works divides them into literary works (primarily novels), critical essays, and fragmentary or philosophical works, though there is argument as to how we must understand "philosophy" in Blanchot's terms, and few would argue that the divisions among the works are always neat or obvious.

4. SNB, 1.

"La mort, nous n'y sommes pas habitués." PAD, 7.

5. WD, 11.

"Le silence est impossible. C'est pourquoi nous le désirons." ED, 23.

6. See Blanchot, "As if there would have reverberated, in a muffled way, a call." SNB, 7.

"Comme si eût retenti, d'une manière étoufée, un appel." PAD, 15.

7. WD, 6.

"Le désastre, nous le connaissons peut-être sous d'autres noms peut-être joyeux . . ." ED, 15.

8. "And if they speak, it is with the voice of others, a voice always other than theirs which somehow accuses them, interrogates and obliges them to answer for a silent affliction which they bear without awareness." WD, 22.

". . . et que s'ils parlent, c'est par la voix des autres, une voix toujours autre qui en quelque sorte les accuse, les met en cause, les obligeant à répondre d'un malheur silencieux qu'ils portent sans conscience." ED, 40.

9. Maurice Blanchot, *The Infinite Conversation*, translated by Susan Hanson (Minneapolis: University of Minnesota Press, 1993), xxiii. Hereafter, IC.

". . . la pause légitime, celle permettant le tour à tour des conversations, la pause bienveillante, intelligente, ou encore la belle attente par laquelle deux interlocuteurs, d'une rive à l'autre, mesurent leur droit à communiquer." *L'Entretien infini* (Paris: Gallimard, 1969), xxvi. Hereafter, EI.

10. IC, 48.

"Toute parole commençante commence par répondre, réponse à ce qui n'est pas encore entendu, réponse elle-même attentive où s'affirme l'attente impatiente de l'inconnu et l'espoir désirant de la présence." EI, 69.

11. Maurice Blanchot, "Waiting," translated by Michael Holland, *The Blanchot reader*, 273.

"l'Attente," in *Martin Heidegger Zum Siebzigsten Geburtstag* (Pfullingen, Neske, 1959). I have not been able to find the original version of this essay.

12. "One can write it once, live it once . . . what happens when madness comes back a second time? One would have the right to think oneself better defended, facing a more familiar adversary. . . . However, one thinks only of this one thing: what had been impossible—madness—even in the memory one retains of it, is possible again. . . ." SNB, 103.

"On peut l'écrire une fois, le vivre une fois . . . mais qu'arrive-t-il, lorsque celle-ci revient un seconde fois? On aurait le droit de se croire mieux défendu. . . . Seulement, on ne pense plus qu'à une chose: ce qui a été impossible—la folie—même dans le souvenir qu'on garde d'elle, est à nouveau possible. . . ." PAD, 142.

13. SNB, 45.

"A la rigueur, nous maintenons ce mot en position interrogative : Hölderlin était fou, mais l'était-il?" "La folie serait ainsi un mot en perpétuelle disconvenance avec lui-même et interrogatif de part en part, tel qu'il mettrait en question sa possibilité et, par lui, la possibilité du langage qui le comporterait, donc l'interrogation, elle aussi. . . ." PAD, 65.

14. See the introduction to Michel Foucault, *Madness and Civilization* (London: Routledge, 1989): "In the serene world of mental illness, modern man no longer communicates with the madman. . . . As for a common language, there is no such thing, or rather there is no such thing any longer; the constitution of madness as mental illness, at the end of the eighteenth century, affords the evidence of a broken dialogue, posits the separation as already effected, and thrusts into oblivion all those stammered, imperfect words without fixed syntax in which the exchange between madness and reason was made. The language of psychiatry, which is a monologue of reason *about* madness, has been established only on the basis of such a silence." x–xi, introduction to English translation only; originally published as *Folie et Deraison*, (Paris: Plon, 1971).

Also: "This dialogue itself was now disengaged; silence was absolute; there was no longer any common language . . . the language of delirium can be answered only by an absence of language . . . it refers, in an ultimately silent awareness, only to transgression. . . . In this inveterate silence, transgression has taken over the very sources of speech." Ibid., 262.

15. IC, 198.

". . . ce qui se constitue en silence, dans la réclusion du Grand Renfermement, par un mouvement qui répond au bannissement prononcé par Descartes, c'est le monde même de la Déraison . . . les prohibitions sexuelles, les interdits religieux, tous les excès de la pensée et du cœur." EI, 295.

16. IC, 197.

". . . la folie révèle une profondeur bouleversante, un violence souterraine et comme un savoir démesuré, ravageur et secret . . ." EI, 293.

17. WD, 7.

"Je dirai plutôt: rien d'extrême que par la douceur." ED, 16.

18. IC, 79.

"Nous avons d'abord deux grandes distinctions . . . la pause qui permet l'échange; l'attente qui mesure la distance infinie. Mais avec l'attente, ce n'est pas seulement la belle rupture préparant l'acte poétique qui s'affirme, mais aussi, et en même temps, d'autre formes de cessation, très profondes, très perverses, de plus en plus perverses, et toujours telles que si on le distingue, cette distinction n'écarte pas, mais postule l'ambiguïté." EI, 112.

19. Heidegger, too, emphasizes waiting, for death primarily; his sense of the impossible passivity of the wait, however, seems to be less complex than Blanchot's.

20. ". . . in time, waiting comes to an end without being put to an end by waiting." "Waiting," 274.

21. SNB, 90.

"La mort, ce mot mal unifié, interrogation toujours déplacée." PAD, 125.

22. "Waiting," 276.

23. Leslie Hill writes, "The question of the possibility or impossibility of death, in Blanchot, is never far from the question of language; indeed, the two in Blanchot are largely indissociable, if not in fact synonymous." MBEC, 170. On this issue compare Jacques Derrida, *Aporias*, translated by Thomas Dutoit (Stanford: Stanford University Press, 1993). For Derrida as for Blanchot, this concern arises and then diverges from a concern with Heideggerian being-toward-death.

24. SNB, 67. "'Entre dans l'élément destructeur,', nous n'écrivons pas un mot qui ne contienne cette invitation et, parfois, celle-ci qui est superflue: laisse-toi te détruire." PAD, 95.

25. SNB, 90.

"Parler, c'est perdre plutôt que retenir; confier à l'oubli plutôt qu'à la mémoire. . . ." PAD, 124.

26. SNB, 90.

". . . l'écriture est toujours seconde, en ce sens que, même si rien ne la précède, elle ne se pose pas pour première, ruinant plutôt, par un renvoi indéfini qui ne laisse pas de place au vide même, toute primauté. Telle est alors, à peine indiquée, la violence dispersée de l'écriture, une violence par laquelle la parole est toujours déjà mise à l'écart, effacée par avance et non plus restaurée, violence qui, il est vrai, n'est pas naturelle et nous empêche aussi, mourant, de mourir d'une mort naturelle." PAD , 125.

27. WD, 8.

". . . il n'y a silence qu'écrit, réserve déchirée, entaille qui rend impossible le détail." ED, 19.

28. IC, 28.

"Le jeu de l'étymologie courante fait de l'écriture un mouvement coupant, une déchirure, un crise . . . l'outil propre à écrire qui était aussi propre à inciser: le stylet."

". . . ce rappel incisif évoque une opération tranchante, sinon une boucherie: une sorte de violence. . . ." EI, 38–39.

29. IC, 29.

". . . parler, c'est puiser au fond de la parole l'oubli qui est l'inépuisable." EI, 40.

30. "Waiting," 272.

31. Hill, MBEC, 61.

32. "Let us think of the obscure combat between language and presence. . . ." SNB, 31.

"Évoquons l'obscur combat entre langage et présence . . ." PAD, 46.

33. SNB, 46.

"Que la folie soit présente dans tout langage ne suffit pas à établir qu'elle n'y est pas omise." PAD, 67.

34. This is most conspicuously true for speaking, in which the voice is not identical with the words it speaks. See IC, 258: "The voice frees not only from representation, but also, in advance, from meaning, without, however, succeeding in doing more than committing itself to the ideal madness of delirium."

"La voix libère non seulement de la représentation, mais, par avance, du sens, sans cependant réussir à faire plus que de se confier à la folie idéale du délire." EI, 386.

35. WD, 52.

"Le mot, presque privé de sens, est bruyant. Le sens est silence limité (la parole est relativement silencieuse, dans la mesure où elle porte ce en quoi elle s'absente, le sens déjà absent, penchant vers l'asémique)." ED, 87.

36. IC, 214.

"[La parole] est périssable. A peine dite, elle s'efface, elle se perd sans recours. Elle s'oublie." EI, 317.

37. SNB, 31.

"C'est . . . en luttant pour la présence (en acceptant de se faire naïvement le mémorial de quelque chose qui s'y présente) que le langage la détruit perfidement. Cela arrive par l'écriture." PAD, 47.

38. Unworking or worklessness (désouvrement) is, approximately, the defiance of the finality of the work, the recognition in the work of what cannot be in the work, its necessary outside, its contraries and contradictions.

39. Michael Newman, "The trace of trauma," in *Maurice Blanchot: The Demand of Writing*, edited by Carolyn Bailey Gill (London: Routledge, 1996), 156–57.

40. WD, 53.

"Que ce qui s'écrit résonne dans le silence, le faisant résonner longtemps, avant de retourner à la paix immobile où veille encore l'énigme." ED, 88.

41. WD, 23.

". . . le mourir qui m'est, quoique sans partage, commun avec tous." ED, 42.

42. WD, 118.

"S'il est vrai que, pour un certain Freud, 'Notre inconscient ne saurait se représenter notre propre mortalité,' cela signifie tout au plus que mourir est irreprésentable, non pas seulement parce que mourir est sans présent, mais parce qu'il n'a pas de lieu, fût-ce dans le temps, la temporalité du temps." ED, 181.

43. SNB, 44.

"La violence est au travail dans le langage et, plus décidément, dans la parole d'écriture, pour autant que le langage se dérobe au travail: cette action de se dérober appartient encore à la violence." PAD, 65.

44. See Bataille, *Erotism*, 186. Cf. Deleuze, writing of Freud's *Beyond the Pleasure Principle* in *Masochism: Coldness and Cruelty*, translated by Jean McNeil (New York: Zone Books, 1991), 116: ". . . Thanatos, the groundless, supported and brought to the surface by Eros, remains absolutely silent. . . ."

". . . Thanatos, le sans-fond porté par Éros, ramené à la surface, est essentielle-ment silencieux. . . ." *Présentation de Sacher-Masoch: Le Froid et le Cruel* (Paris: Minuit, 1967), 100.

45. IC, 34.

". . . nous avons perdu la mort. . . . Nous le nommons, mais pour le maîtriser par un nom et, en ce nom, à la fin nous en défaire." EI, 47.

46. See introduction, note 24.

47. WD, 76.

"Nous devons passer par ce savoir et l'oublier." ED, 122.

48. SNB, 11.

"Sache seulement—injonction que ne se présente pas—que la loi du retour, valant pour tout le passe et pour tout l'avenir, ne te permettra jamais, sauf par un malentendu, de te laisser une place dans un présent possible, ni de laisser nulle présence venir jusqu'à toi." PAD, 20.

49. SNB, 41.

"L'Éternel Retour du Même: l'avoir été, répétition d'un aura lieu comme ayant été, ne fait signe à nulle présence, fût-elle de jadis. L'Éternel Retour dirait cela, il dirait que, dans l'avoir été, nul présente ne se retient, sauf en ce dire, s'il se disait." PAD, 61.

50. "Memory is the gathering of thought upon what everywhere demands to be thought about first of all. Memory is the gathering of recollection, thinking back. It safely keeps and keeps concealed within it that to which at each given time thought must first be given in everything that essentially is. . . ." "What Calls for Thinking?" MHBW, 352.

"Gedächtnis ist die Versammlung des Denkens auf das, was überall im voraus schon bedacht sein möchte. Gedächtnis ist die Versammlung des Andenkens. Sie birgt bei sich und verbirgt in sich das, woran jeweils zuvor zu denken ist bei allem, was west und sich als Wesendes, Gewesendes zuspricht. . . ." WHD, 7.

51. WD, 25.

". . . nous rapportant à un passé sans mémoire." ED, 45.

52. SNB, 112.

"Je ne sais pas, mais je pressens que je vais avoir su." PAD, 153.

53. IC, 275.

". . . l'éternité du retour—son infini—ne permet pas d'assigner à la figure un centre et pas davantage une infinité de centres, de même que l'infini de la répétition ne saurait se totaliser jusqu'à produire l'unité d'une figure strictement délimitée et dont la constitution échapperait à la loi qu'elle figure. Si l'Éternel Retour peut s'affirmer, il n'affirme ni le retour comme cercle, ni la primauté de l'Un, ni le Tout, fût-ce sous la nécessité que, par l'Éternel Retour, 'tout revient', . . . ce n'est pas le Tout qui revient, mais: cela revient, le retour (comme neutre) revient." EI, 411.

54. WD, 105.

"Oubli, souvenir de l'immémorial, sans mémoire." ED, 163.

55. IC, 314.

". . . l'Oubli est la divinité primordiale, l'aïeul vénérable, la première présence de ce qui donnera lieu, par une génération plus tardive, à Mnémosyne, . . . L'essence de la mémoire est ainsi l'oubli, cet oubli où il faut boire pour mourir." EI, 460.

56. See WD, 76; ED, 122.

57. SNB, 10.

"L'a t-il donc oubliée, la rencontre toujours à venir qui cependant a toujours déjà eu lieu, dans un passé éternel, éternellement sans présent?" PAD, 20.

58. SNB, 54. PAD, 72.

59. IC 195.

". . . l'oubli échappe. Cela ne signifie pas simplement qu'une possibilité, par l'oubli, nous est ôtée, et une certaine impuissance révélée, mais que la possibilité qu'est l'oubli est glissement hors de la possibilité." EI, 290.

Cf WD, 28: "Passive: the un-story, that which escapes quotation and which memory does not recall—forgetfulness as thought. That which, in other words, cannot be forgotten because it has always already fallen outside memory."

"Passif: le non-récit, ce qui échappe à la citation et que le souvenir ne rappellerait pas—l'oubli comme pensé, c'est-à-dire ce qui ne saurait être oublié parce que toujours déjà tombé hors mémoire." ED, 49.

60. At WD 14, Blanchot tells us of "the silent rupture of the fragmentary."

". . . la rupture silencieuse du fragmentaire." ED, 30.

61. WD, 109.

"[L]a perte impossible . . . ne laisse pas se figer en un système les tensions qui déchirent la pensée et que soutient l'âpreté d'un langage sans repos." ED, 168–69.

62. SNB, 106.

"Cependant, rien n'est dit, si nous ne nous forçons pas à penser . . . la rupture invisible d'interdit, la transgression dont nous nous sentons alors les complices, parce qu'elle est aussi bien notre propre étrangeté . . ." PAD, 146.

63. IC, 159.

"[Fragmentation] a bien 'partie liée' avec la révélation de l'Éternel Retour. L'Éternel Retour dit le temps comme éternelle répétition, et la parole de fragment répète cette répétition en la destituant de toute éternité." EI, 238.

64. WD, 51.

"La vif de la vie, ce serait l'avivement qui ne se contente pas de la présence vivante, qui consume ce qui est présent jusqu'à l'exemption, l'exemplarité . . . de la non-présence . . . l'absence en sa vivacité, toujours revenant sans venue." ED, 86.

65. WD, 117.

"Il n'y a pas d'origine, si origine suppose une présence originelle. Toujours passé, d'ores et déjà passé, quelque chose qui s'est passé sans être présent, voilà l'immémorial que nous donne l'oubli, disant: tout commencement est recommencement." ED, 180.

66. IC, 196.

"Par le mouvement qui dérobe (l'oubli), nous nous laissons tourner vers ce qui échappe (la mort), comme si la seule approche authentique de cet événement inauthentique appartenait à l'oubli. L'oubli, la mort: le détour sans conditions." EI, 291.

67. IC, 196.

". . . dans l'espace qui s'établit entre folie et déraison nous à nous demander s'il est vrai que la littérature et l'art pourraient accueillir ces expériences-limites et, ainsi, préparer, par-delà la culture, un rapport avec ce que rejette la culture: parole des confines, dehors d'écriture." EI, 292.

68. WD, 3.

". . . souvenir par oubli, le dehors à nouveau." ED, 10.

69. SNB, 91.

"désir de ce qui provoque la peur que rien ne provoque." PAD, 126.

70. IC, 53.

". . . la pensée qui pense plus qu'elle ne pense . . ." EI, 76.

71. Ibid.

". . . désir de ce qui ne nous manque pas, désir qui ne peut être satisfait et ne désire pas s'unir avec le désiré: il désire cela dont celui qui doit lui rester inaccessible et étranger . . ." Ibid.

72. IC, 192.

". . . l'espace muet, fermé, où erre sans fin le désir . . ." EI, 288

73. IC, 211.

"cette affirmation . . . dont l'homme ne se souvient pas, . . . mesure d'extrême douleur et d'extrême joie." EI, 313.

74. Deleuze, *Coldness and Cruelty*, "We must conceive of another [form of repetition] which in its turn repeats *what was before the instant*. . . ." "Beyond Eros we encounter Thanatos; beyond the ground, the abyss of the groundless; beyond the repetition that links, the repetition that erases and destroys." 114.

"Comment la répétition jouerait-elle un *en même temps* (en même temps que l'excitation, en même temps que la vie) sans jouer aussi *l'avant*. . . ." "Au-delà d'Éros, Thanatos. Au-delà du fond, le sans-fond. Au-delà de la répétition-lien, la répétition-gomme, qui efface et qui tue." *Présentation de Sacher-Mascoch*, 98–99.

75. SNB, 1.

"Entrons dans ce rapport." PAD, 7.

76. WD, 47.

"Dans l'intensité mortelle, le silence fuyant du cri innombrable." ED, 80.

77. IC, 193.

"Léthé est aussi le compagnon d'Éros, l'éveil propre au sommeil, cela, l'écart, dont il n'y a pas à s'écarter, puisqu'il vient en tout ce qui s'écarte . . ." EI, 288. See also the final chapter of the present work.

78. IC, 207.

". . . comme si l'impossibilité, cela en quoi nous ne pouvons plus pouvoir, nous attendait derrière tout ce que nous vivons, pensons et disons, pour peu que nous ayons été une fois au bout de cette attente, sans jamais manquer à ce qu'a exigé ce surplus, ce surcroît, surplus de vide, surcroît de 'négativité' qui est en nous le cœur infini de la passion de la pensée." EI, 308.

79. Bataille, IE, 51.

"Le plus étrange est que le non-savoir ait une sanction. Comme si, du dehors, il nous était dit: «Enfin te voici.»" L'EI, 65.

chapter two

1. Compare Blanchot on Kafka: "When Kafka allows a friend to understand that he writes because otherwise he would go mad, he knows that writing is madness already. . . . Madness against madness, then." WD, 43.

"Quand Kafka laisse entendre à un ami qu'il écrit parce que, autrement, il deviendrait fou, il sait qu'écrire est déjà folie. . . . Folie contre folie. . . ." ED, 74.

2. Stamelman, in EJSB, 92.

3. Maurice Blanchot, "The Essential Solitude," in *The space of literature*, translated by Ann Smock (Lincoln: University of Nebraska Press, 1982), 23.

"La solitude essentielle," in *L'espace littéraire* (Paris: Gallimard, 1955), 13.

4. "Profound communication demands silence. In the end, action, which predication signifies, is limited to this: closing one's door in order to stop discourse (the noise, the mechanics of the outside).

The door must remain open and shut at the same time." IE, 92.

"La communication profonde veut le silence. En dernier lieu, l'action, que la prédication signifie, se limite à ceci: fermer sa porte afin d'arrêter le discours (le bruit, la mécanique du dehors).

La porte en même temps doit demeurer ouverte et fermée." L'EI, 109.

5. See Sigmund Freud, "The unconscious," in *General Psychological Theory*, edited by Philip Rieff (NY: Macmillan, 1963) 121, 135.

"Das Unbewußte," (1915), in *Studienausgabe, Bd. III, Psychologie des Unbewußten* (Frankfurt: S. Fischer, 1975), 130, 145–46.

6. See Denis Hollier, introduction to Georges Bataille, *Guilty*, translated by Bruce Boone (Venice CA: Lapis Press, 1988), xii.

7. In Nietzsche the role of intensity is especially clear in the play between pleasure and displeasure. See particularly GS/ FW, e.g., secs. 12, 127, 301.

8. For Sade, intensity is of far greater importance than what we more generally recognize as pleasure, and the philosophical significance of intensity may be what links Sade and Nietzsche, possibly explaining the interest of so many of the French Nietzscheans in Sade's indigestible prose.

9. Michel Foucault, "Preface to Transgression," in *Language countermemory practice*, translated by Donald F. Bouchard and Sherry Simon (Ithaca: Cornell University Press, 1977), 43.

"Cette fracture du sujet philosophique, elle n'est pas seulement rendue sensible par la juxtaposition d'oeuvres romanesques et de textes de réflexion dans le langage de notre pensée. L'oeuvre de Bataille la montre de bien plus près, dans un perpétuel passage à des niveaux différents de parole, par un décrochage systématique par rapport au Je que vient de prendre la parole, prêt déjà à la déployer et à s'installer en elle: décrochages dans le temps . . . décrochage dans la distance de la parole à celui qui parle (journal, carnets, poèmes, récites, méditations, discours démonstratifs), décrochages intérieurs à la souveraineté qui pense et écrit (livres, textes anonymes, préface à ses propres livres, notes ajoutées)." "Préface à la transgression," *Critique* , August/ September 1963, 761.

10. Cited in Lionel Abel, "Georges Bataille and the Repetition of Nietzsche," in *On Bataille: Critical Essays*, edited and translated by Leslie Anne Boldt-Irons (Albany: SUNY Press, 1995), 57. Hereafter, OBCE. This line is given as a quotation from Inner Experience, without page citation. I have not succeeded in tracking it down.

11. IE, 13.

"son petit tassement." L'EI, 25.

12. See *Erotism*, "Of all problems eroticism is the most mysterious, the most general, and the least straightforward. . . . The erotic moment is also the most intense of

all (except perhaps for mystical experience); hence its place is at the loftiest peak of man's spirit. . . . I believe that the supreme philosophical question coincides with the summits of eroticism." 273.

"Entre tous les problèmes, *L'Érotisme* est le plus mystérieux, le plus général, le plus à l'écart. . . . Le moment érotique est aussi le plus intense (excepté, si l'on veut, l'expérience des mystiques). Ainsi est-il situé au sommet de l'esprit humain. . . . La suprême interrogation philosophique coïncide, je le pense, avec le sommet de *L'Éro-tisme*." *L'Érotisme*, 301–02.

13. IE, 92.

"l'extase elle-même est vide envisagée comme exercice privé, n'important que pour un seul." L'EI, 109.

14. *Erotism*, 271.

"perdu dans le silence sans fin," *L'Érotisme*, 297. See also Foucault, noting Bataille's effort "to kill God in order to lose language in a deafening night and because this wound must make him bleed until there springs forth 'an immense alleluia lost in the interminable silence'—and this is communication." "Preface to Transgression," 32.

"Tuer Dieu pour perdre le langage dans une nuit assourdissante, et parce que cette blessure doit le fair saigner jusqu'à ce que jaillisse un «immense alléluia perdu dans le silence sans fin» (c'est la communication)." "Préface à la transgression," 753.

15. IE, 50.

"L'extrême est ailleurs. Il n'est entièrement atteint que communiqué . . ." L'EI, 64.

16. Ibid.

"Quand l'extrême est là, les moyens qui servent à l'atteindre n'y sont plus." Ibid.

17. "Of the Simulacrum in Georges Bataille's Communication," OBCE, 150.

18. Foucault, "Preface to Transgression," 39.

"Le langage de Bataille en revanche s'effondre sans cesse au coeur de son propre espace, laissant à nu, dans l'inertie de l'extase, le sujet insistant et visible qui a tenté de le tenir à bout de bras, et se trouve comme rejeté par lui, exténué sur le sable de ce qui'il ne puet plus dire." "Preface à la transgression," 759.

19. Ibid., 40.

"La possibilité d'une telle pensée ne nous vient-elle pas en effet, dans un langage qui justement nous la dérobe comme pensée et la reconduit jusqu'à l'impossibilité même du langage? Jusqu'à cette limite où vient en question l'être du langage?" Ibid., 759.

20. IE, 16. L'EI, 28.

21. See Georges Bataille, "The Sorcerer's Apprentice," in *Visions of Excess*, edited by Allan Stoekel, translated by Allan Stoekel, Carl R. Lovitt, and Donald M. Leslie, Jr. (Minneapolis: University of Minnesota Press, 1985), 223. I have not found this essay in the French.

22. *Guilty*, 8.

"De cette manière, j'en viens à la fin du langage qu'est la mort. En puissance, il s'agit encore d'un langage, mais dont le sens—déjà l'absence de sens—est donné das les mots qui mettent fin au langage. Ces mots n'ont de sens, du moins, que dans la mesure où ils précèdent immédiatement le silence (le silence qui met fin): ils n'au-raient de sens plein qu'*oubliés*, tombant décidément, subitement, dans l'oubli." *Le Coupable* (Paris: Gallimard, 1944), xiii–xiv. Hereafter, LC.

23. *Erotism*, 186.

". . . le langage étant, par définition, l'expression de l'homme civilisé, la violence est silencieuse. . . . *La violence est silencieuse et le langage de Sade est paradoxal.* Le lan-gage commun se refuse à l'expression de la violence . . ." *L'Érotisme*, 206.

24. *Erotism*, 187.

"Mais le silence ne supprime pas ce dont le langage ne peut être l'affirmation : la violence n'est pas moins irréductible que la mort, et si le langage dérobe par un biais l'universel anéantissement—l'oeuvre sereine du *temps*—le langage seul en souffre, en est limité, non le temps, non la violence." *L'Érotisme*, 207.

25. IE, 150.

"Ce qu'on ne saisit pas: que la littérature n'étant rien si elle n'est poésie étant le contraire de son nom, le langage littéraire—expression des désirs cachés, de la vie que l'érotisme n'est celle des fonctions sexuelles. D'où la «terreur» sévissant à la fin «dans les lettres», comme la recherche de vices, d'excitations nouvelles, à fin de la vie d'un débauché." L'EI, 173.

26. Foucault, "Preface to Transgression," 30. "Préface à la transgression," 752.

27. *Guilty*, 53.

". . . je ne puis rien écrire qui n'ait l'allure d'un pas menant à la mort. C'es la seule cohésion, de notes fébriles, auxquelles il n'est pas d'autre explication." LC, 67.

28. Jean-Louis Baudry, "Bataille and Science: Introduction to Inner Experience," in OBCE, 269.

29. *Erotism*, 275.

"Donner à la philosophie la transgression pour fondement . . . , c'est substituer au langage une contemplation silencieuse. . . . Le langage n'a nullement disparu. Le som-met serait-il accessible si le discours n'en avait révélé les accès? Mais le langage qui les décrivit n'a plus de sens à l'instant décisif quand la transgression elle-même en son mouvement se substitue l'exposé discursif de la transgression, mais un moment suprême s'ajoute à ces apparitions successives . . ." *L'Érotisme*, 303.

30. Georges Bataille, *Theory of Religion*, translated by Robert Hurley (NY: Zone Books, 1992), 50–51, my italics. Hereafter, TR.

"Est intime, au sens fort, ce qui a l'emportement d'une absence d'individualité, la sonorité insaisissable d'un fleuve, la vide limpidité du ciel: c'est encore un définition négative, à laquelle l'essentiel fait défaut.

Ces énoncés ont la valuer vague d'inaccessibles lointains, mais en contrepartie les définitions articulées substituent l'arbre à la forêt, l'articulation distincte à ce qui est articulé.

Je recourrai néanmoins à l'articulation.

Paradoxalement, l'intimité est la violence, et elle est la destruction, parce qu'elle n'est pas compatible avec la position de l'individu séparé. Si l'on décrit l'individu dans l'opération du sacrifice, il se définit par l'angoisse. Mais si le sacrifice est angoissant, c'est que l'individu y prend part." *Théorie de la religion* (Paris: Gallimard, 1973), 68–69. Hereafter, TdR.

31. *Guilty*, 28–9.

"Il n'est pas moins pusillanime de redouter la stabilité fondamentale que d'hésiter à la rompre. . . . Déséquilibre, *sacrifice* sont autant plus grands que leur object était en équilibre, qu'il éait *achevé*. Ces principes s'opposent à la morale nécessairement niveleuse, . . . Ils ruinent la morale romantique du désordre autant que la morale contraire." LC, 33.

32. TR, 13.

"L'inévitable inachèvement ne ralentit en aucune mesure la réponse qui est un movement—fût-il en un sens absence de réponse. Au contrarie, il lui donne la vérité de cri de l'impossible." TdR, 20.

We might note that the principles of life and language share the same methodological demand:

"[I]n principle the means are always double. On the one hand, one appeals to the excess of forces, to movements of intoxication, of desire. And on the other hand, in order to have at one's disposal a quantity of forces, one mutilates oneself (through ascesis . . .)" IE, 23.

". . . les moyens sont en principe toujours doubles. D'une part, on fait appel à l'excès des forces, à des mouvements d'ivresse, de désir. Et d'autre part, afin de disposer de forces en quantité, on se mutile (par l'ascèse . . .)" L'EI, 35–36.

33. See Blanchot: "*Mad language* would be, in any speech, not only the possibility that would make it speak at the risk of making it non-speaking (risk without which it would not speak), but the limit that detains all language and which, never fixed in advance, nor theoretically determinable, still less such that once could write: 'there is a limit,' thus outside of any 'there is', could inscribe itself only on the basis of its own crossing—the crossing of the uncrossable—and, from this, prohibited." "That madness is present in every language is not enough to establish that it is not omitted in them." SNB, 45–46.

"*La langage fou* serait, en toute parole, non seulement la possibilité qui la ferait parler au risque de la rendre non-parlante (risque sans lequel elle ne parlerait pas), mais la limite qui détient toute langue et qui, jamais fixée à l'avance, ni théoriquement déterminable, encore moins telle qu'on pourrait écrire: «il y a une limite», donc hors de tout «il y a», ne saurait s'inscrire qu'à partir de son franchissement—le franchissement de l'infranchissable—et, à partir de là, interdit." "Que la folie soit présente dans tout langage ne suffit pas à établir qu'elle n'y est pas omise." PAD 66, 67.

34. *Erotism*, 40–41.

". . . ce Dieu dont nous voudrons former la notion saisissable ne cesse pas, excédant cette notion, d'excéder les limites de la raison. Dans le domaine de notre vie, l'excès se manifeste dans la mesure où la violence l'emporte sur la raison." *L'Érotisme*, 46.

35. *Guilty*, 27.

" il imagine Dieu lui'même succombant au désir de l'inachèvement, au désir d'être un homme et pauvre, et de mourir dans un supplice." LC, 30.

36. IE, 131.

". . . me voici Dieu, ignorance inconnue, inconnaissable." L'EI, 152.

37. Antonin Artaud, in *The Artaud Anthology*, edited by Jack Hirschman, various translators (San Francisco: City Lights Books, 1965), 51. Hereafter, AA.

"Tout ce qui dans l'ordre des choses écrites abondone le domaine de la perception ordonnée et claire, tout ce qui vise à créer un renversement des apparences, à introduire un doute sur la position des images de l'esprit les unes par rapport aux autres, tout ce qui provoque la confusion sans détruire la force de la pensée jaillissante, tout ce qui renverse les rapports des choses en donnant à la pensée bouleversée un aspect encore plus grand de vérité et de violence, tout cela offre une issue la mort, nous met en rapport avec des états plus affinés de l'esprit au sein desquels la mort s'exprime." "L'Art et la mort," in *L'ombilic des limbes*, (Paris: Gallimard, 1956), 135. Hereafter, OL.

38. AA, 37.

"Je suis celui qui a le mieux senti le désarroi stupéfiant de sa langue dans ses relations avec la pensée. Je suis celui qui a le mieux repéré la minute de ses plus intimes, de ses plus insoupçonnables glissements." OL, 105.

39. AA, 36.

"Je suis imbécile, par suppression de pensée, par malformation de pensée, je suis vacant par stupéfaction de ma langue." OL, 102.

40. AA, 32.

"J'ai senti vraiment que vous rompiez autour de moi l'atmosphère, que vous faisiez le vide pour me permettre d'avancer, pour donner la place d'un espace impossible à ce qui en moi n'était encore qu'en puissance, à toute une germination virtuelle, et qui devait naître, aspirée par la place qui s'offrait.

Je me suis mis souvent dans cet état d'absurde impossible, pour essayer de faire naître en moi de la pensée." OL, 87.

41. AA, 26.

"Ce livre je le mets en suspension dans la vie, je veux qu'il soit mordu par les choses extérieures, et d'abord par tous les soubresauts en cisaille, toutes les cillations de *mon moi à venir*." OL, 51.

42. IE, 38.

"Je ne puis concevoir ma vie désormais, sinon clouée à *l'extrême du possible.* . . . (Mais que faire? oublier? aussitôt, je le sens, je serai fou: on comprend mal encore la misère d'un esprit dévêtu.)" L'EI, 51.

43. *Guilty*, 82.

"Si la faculté discursive intervient, la limite du possible est sa seule limite." LC, 112.

chapter three

1. Plato, *Republic*, in *The collected dialogues of Plato*, edited by Edith Hamilton and Huntington Cairns (Princeton: Princeton University Press, 1961), books II–III. Of course, the attitude toward poetry is, throughout this work, complex; its own artfulness, Socrates's persistent use of poetic allusion, and the concessions of book X all suggest that a simple and straightforward reading of the *Republic* is likely to miss much.

2. Plato, *Phaedrus*, translated by Alexander Nehamas and Paul Woodruff (Indianapolis: Hackett Publishing, 1995), ll. 244B–C. Socrates admits that there is a bit of an etymological trick in this derivation; prophecy, *mantic*, must drop its *t* to be identified with *mania*, madness. See ibid., 244D.

3. Ibid., 245A.

4. Ibid., 230D.

5. Ibid., 275 D–E.

6. In this condemnation of chatter, Celan's speech obviously invokes for us Heidegger (see *Being and Time*, sec. 34, and "What calls for thinking?"), with whom his relation is understandably quite uncomfortable, given Heidegger's support of National Socialism.

7. Paul Celan, "The meridian," in *Paul Celan, collected prose*, translated by Rosmarie Waldrop (Riverdale-on-Hudson, NY: Sheep Meadow Press, 1986), 48. Hereafter, PCCP.

"Gewiß, das Gedicht—das Gedicht heute—zeigt, und das hat, glaube ich, denn doch nur mittelbar mit den—nicht zu unterschätzenden—Schwierigkeiten der Wortwahl, dem rapideren Gefälle der Syntax oder dem wacheren Sinn für die Ellipse zu tun,—das Gedicht zeigt, das ist unverkennbar, eine starke Niegung zum Verstummen." "Der Meridian," in *Paul Celan: Der Meridian und andere Prose* (Frankfurt: Suhrkamp, 1983), 54. Hereafter, PCDM.

8. TBR, vol. 3, 74.

«Dieu Se retira du monde non pour y installer l'homme mais la parole . . .» LR, 368.

9. Ibid.

"Il savait que celle-ci s'arrogerait d'office le droit d'annexer l'univers. Et aussi parce qu'il ne pouvait se résoudre à renoncer tout à fait à Son roynaume." Ibid.

10. Edmond Jabès, "There is such a thing as Jewish writing," translated by Rosmarie Waldrop, in EJSB, 28.

11. TBR, vol. 3, 13.

"Un hors-temps est le temps du livre à son prélude . . . un écho étouffé à l'écho." LR, 297.

12. TBR, vol. 3, 79.

"La mémoire est promesse d'avenir. «Dis-moi ce dont tu te souviens et je te dirai qui tu seras», écrivait reb Horel, l'un des rabbins imaginaires. . . .

—Peut-on se souvenir d'un lieu où l'on n'a pas séjourné, d'un visage que l'on n'a pas approché, d'un object qu'à aucun moment on n'a saisi?, demandait reb Zaoud à reb Bécri.—Je me souviens bien de Dieu, répondit celui-ci." LR, 375.

13. Paul Auster, "An interview with Edmond Jabès," in EJSB, 13. The quotation is Jabès's; the ellipses are in the original.

14. TBR, vol. 3, 44–45.

". . . ce qui continue, ici, de sécrire ne s'écrit que dans un passé duquel je ne puis me porter garant; un passé qui fut, pourtant, un présent permanent jusqu'à la décisive rupture qu'il m'est impossible de situer dans le temps, car je suis sans memoire et sans paroles et que là où je tente, avec de plus en plus de difficultés, de me mouvoir encore, il n'y a pas de temps." LR, 333–34.

15. Edmond Jabès, *The little book of unsuspected subversion*, translated by Rosmarie Waldrop (Stanford: Stanford University Press, 1996), 58. Hereafter, LBUS.

"Purité du silence! Non pas du silence qui sait, qui a entendu et répété; mais du silence qui a oublié." *Le petit livre de la subversion hors de soupçon* (Paris: Gallimard, 1982), 64. Hereafter, PLSHS.

16. Jabès, TBR 1, 48.

"Dieu parle dans l'oubli. Sa parole est oubli. Elle est parole d'oubli de toute parole." LR, 70.

17. Edmond Jabès, "The question of displacement into the lawfulness of the book," translated by Rosmarie Waldrop, in EJSB, 229.

18. *The Holy Bible, New International Version* (NY: Harper Collins, 1984), Genesis, 1:3–27.

19. Ibid., John 1:1.

20. Jabès, TBR, vol. 3, 74.

"L'homme n'a aucun besoin d'infini. . . . Ce sont pensées, paroles, vocables qui, toujours en quête dépassement, en subissent la fatale fascination." LR, 368.

21. Ibid.,13.

"La lisibilité—du livre—est liée au temps—du livre." LR, 297.

22. Ibid., 67–68.

"Livre indéchiffré de Dieu dans le livre décrypté de l'homme où toute parole, dans le silence blessé où elle baigne, mime l'agonie d'une parole originaire dont l'oubli ne serait que l'espace blanc de son destin divin; silence à ses confins, attardé dans l'infini silence." LR, 362.

23. Jabès, LBUS, 43.

"Silencieuse est la Parole de Dieu depuis le jour où, pour se faire entendre, Il a imposé silence à nos paroles humaines, oubliant que c'était à travers elles qu'Il nous parlait.

Le silence de la Parole de Dieu n'est jamais que le silence infini de nos communes paroles terrassées.

Nous ne pouvons atteindre au silence de Dieu qu'en épousant, nous-mêmes, ce silence. La reconnaissance de la Parole de Dieu ne serait donc, pour nous, que l'acceptation de notre propre silence.

Dire ce silence, c'est dire le sacré; mais c'est, également, l'abolir aussitôt." PLSHS, 49–50.

24. TBR 1, 48.

"un mot avant ou après un mot, dans le passé ou dans l'avenir; un mot inutile donc, dont l'emploi chaque l'esprit." LR, 71.

25. TBR 1, 103.

«Si Dieu est, Soi-même, un mot absent, ou, plutôt, s'Il est l'absence du mot, chaque vocable ne serait-il, alors, que le décalque de cette absence?»

L'exploitation de l'absence est langage divin.

Tu écris sur Dieu." LR, 138–39.

26. LBUS, 75.

"«Écrire, disait-il, est un acte de silence dirigé contre le silence . . .»," PLSHS, 81.

27. Jabès in Paul Auster, "An interview with Edmond Jabès," in EJSB, 13–14.

28. Richard Stamelman, "Nomadic writing: the poetics of exile," in EJSB, 109.

29. Jabès, "The question of displacement into the lawfulness of the book," in EJSB, 234. Emphasis mine.

30. Edward A. Kaplan, "The problematic humanism of Edmond Jabès," EJSB, 122.

31. Christopher Fynsk writes, "Pierre Joris has suggested to me that Celan turned Adorno's remarks concerning Auschwitz and poetry in such a manner as to suggest that only poetry is possible after Auschwitz. Celan's statements in his Bremen address would seem to bear out this reading. Furthermore, if we take 'poetry' in a large sense— that is, as an approach to a reality in and through language that is also found in thought and in each of the arts . . . —then I think we may accept Celan's response as a decisive 'counterword' to Adorno's assertion." "The Realities at stake in a poem:

Celan's Bremen and Darmstadt addresses," in *Word Traces: readings of Paul Celan,* edited by Aris Fioretos (Baltimore: Johns Hopkins University Press, 1994), 164–65.

32. The place where they lay, it has/ a name—it has/ none. They did not lie there. "The Straitening," in PPC, 137.

Der Ort, wo sie lagen, er hat/ einen Namen—er hat/ keinen. Sie lagen nicht dort. "Engführung," PPC, 136.

33. Bianca Rosenthal, *Pathways to Paul Celan: A history of critical responses as a chorus of discordant voices* (NY: Peter Lang Publishing, 1995), 116n. Hereafter, Rosenthal.

34. Rosenthal, 36.

35. "Plashes the fountain," PPC 183.

". . . ihr/ gebetscharfen Messer/ meines/ Schweigens. . . ." "Rauscht der Brunnen," PPC, 182.

36. Of course, as the Babel myth reminds us, the multiplicity of langauge may be connected to its fall. Of this, more in the final chapter.

37. "Poetic mutations of silence: at the nexus of Paul Celan and Osip Mandelstam," in *Word Traces,* 369.

38. "Speech on the occasion of receiving the literature prize of the free Hanseatic city of Bremen," in PCCP, 34–35.

"Das Gedicht kann, da es ja eine Erscheinungsform der Sprache und damit seinem Wesen nach dialogisch ist, eine Flaschenpost sein, aufgegeben in dem—gewiß nicht immer hoffnungsstarken—Glauben, sie könnte irgendwo und irgendwann an Land gespült werden, an Herzland vielleicht. Gedichte sind auch in dieser Weise unterwegs: sie halten auf etwas zu. Worauf? Auf etwas Offenstehendes, Bestzbares, auf ein ansprechbares Du vielleicht . . ." "Ansprache Anlässlich der Entgegennahme des Literaturpreises der freien Hansestadt Bremen," in PCDM, 37.

39. "The straitening," PPC, 137.

The German is less personal: "Nirgends/ fragt es nach dir," "Engführung," PPC, 136.

40. Celan, *The meridian,* PCCP, 49.

"Es ist einsam. . . . Wer es schreibt, bleibt ihm mitgegeben." "Der Meridian," PCDM, 55.

41. Celan, *The meridian,* PCCP, 47.

". . . es ist ein furchtbares Verstummen, es verschlägt ihm—und auch uns—den Atem und das Wort. Dichtung: das kann eine Atemwende bedeuten. Wer weiß, vielleicht legt die Dichtung den Weg—auch den Weg der Kunst—um einer solchen Atemwende willen zurück?" "Der Meridian," PCDM, 52.

42. Celan, *The meridian,* PCCP, 49.

"Es behauptet sich—erlauben Sie mir, nach so vielen extremen Formulierungen, nun auch diese—das Gedicht behauptet sich am Rande seiner selbst; es ruft und holt sich, um bestehen zu können, unausgesetzt aus seinem Schon-nicht-mehr in sein Immer-noch Zurück. Dieses Immer-noch kann doch wohl nur ein Sprechen sein." "Der Meridian," PCDM, 54.

43. Celan, *The meridian*, PCCP, 49.

"Das Gedicht will zu einem Andern, es braucht dieses Andere, es braucht ein Gegenüber. Es sucht es auf, es spricht sich ihm zu." "Der Meridian," PCDM, 55.

44. Celan, *The meridian*, PCCP, 50.

". . . es wird verzweifeltes Gespräch." "Der Meridian," PCDM, 56.

45. Aris Fioretos, "Nothing: history and materiality in Celan," in *Word Traces*, 331.

46. Celan, *The meridian*, PCCP, 50.

"Erst im Raum dieses Gesprächs konstituiert sich das Angesprochene, versammelt es sich um das es ansprechende und nennende Ich. Aber in diese Gegenwart bringt das Angesprochene und durch Nennung gleichsam zum Du Gewordene auch sein Anderssein mit." "Der Meridian," PCDM, 56.

47. "Below," PPC, 111.

"Und das Zuviel meiner Rede:/ angelagert dem kleinen/ Kristall in der Tracht deines Schweigens." "Unten," PPC, 110.

48. Paul Celan, "The silicified saying," in *Breathturn*, translated by Pierre Joris (LA: Sun and Moon Press, 1995), 192.

"Den verkieselten Spruch in der Faust, / vergißt du, daß du vergißt,//am Handgelenk schießen/ blinken die Satzzeichen an,/ . . . dort, bei/ der Opferstaude,/ wo das Gedächtnis entbrennt. . . ." ibid., "Den verkieselten Spruch," 193.

49. "Dumb autumn smells," PPC, 171.

"Eine fremde Verlorenheit war/ gestalthaft zugegen, du hüttest/ beinah/ gelebt." "Stumme Herbstgerüche," PPC, 170.

50. Compare also: "I rode through the snow, do you hear/ I rode God into farness—nearness, he sang. . . ." "Over wine and lostness" PPC, 155.

"ich ritt durch die Schnee, hörst du,/ ich ritt Gott in die Ferne—die Nähe, er sang. . . ." "Bei Wein und Verlorenheit," PPC, 154.

51. "You prayer-, you blasphemy-, you/ prayer-sharp knives/ of my/ silence." ". . . Plashes the fountain," PPC, 183.

"Ihr gebet-, ihr lästerungs-, ihr/ gebetscharfen Messer/ meines/ Schweigens." ". . . Rauscht der Brunnen," PPC, 182.

52. "A leaf, treeless," PPC, 331.

"Was sind das für Zeiten, wo ein Gespräch/ beinah ein Verbrechen ist,/ weil es soviel Gesagtes/ mit einschließt?" "Ein Blatt, baumlos," PPC, 330.

53. "Nocturnally pouting," PPC, 91.

"Sie tragen die Schuld ab, die ihren Ursprung beseelte,/ sie tragen sie ab an ein Wort,/ das zu Unrecht besteht, wie der Sommer," "Nächtlich geschürzt," PPC, 90.

54. Rosenthal, 33; reference to Weinrich, Harald, in *Lexikon der Weltliteratur*, edited by Gero von Wilpert (Stuttgart: Kröner, 1963).

55. Rosenthal, 23; reference to Oppens, Kurt, "Gesand und Magie im Zeitalter des Steins. Zur Dichtung Ingeborg Bachmanns und Paul Celans." *Merkuri* 17 #180 (1963), 175–93.

56. "Nothing: history and materiality in Celan," *Word Traces*, 303.

57. Ibid., 316.

58. Christopher Fynsk, "The realities at stake in a poem: Celan's Bremen and Darmstadt addresses," in *Word Traces*, 162.

59. Celan himself was reported to have said this in conversation with Dietlind Meinecke. See "Nothing," *Word Traces*, 316.

60. "Homecoming," from the Elegies, in *Friedrich Hölderlin: poems and fragments*, bilingual edition, translated by Michael Hamburger (Ann Arbor: University of Michigan Press, 1968), 261. Hereafter, PF.

"Nenn' ich den Hohen dabei? Unschikliches liebet ein gott nicht,/ Ihn zu fassen, ist unsere Freude zu klein./ Schweigen müßen wir oft; es fehlen heilige Namen,/ Herzen schlagen und doch bleibet die Rede züruck?" "Heimkunft," PF, 260.

61. "In my boyhood days," PF, 83.

"Ich verstand die Stille des Aethers/ Der Menschen Worte verstand ich nie./. . ./ Im Arme der Götter wuchs ich groß." "Da ich ein Knabe war," PF, 82.

62. "To a priestess of Dessau," PF, 105.

"O theuer warst du, Priesterin! da du dort/ Im Stillen göttlich Feuer behüttest/ Doch theurer heute, da du Zeiten/ Unter den Zeitlichen seegnend feierst." "Am eine Fürstin von Dessau," PF, 104.

63. "Bonaparte," PF, 29.

"Er kann im Gedichte nicht leben und bleiben,/ Er lebt und bleibt in der Welt." "Buonaparte," PF, 28.

64. "To Princess Augusta of Homburg," PF, 111.

"daß von diesem freudigen Tage mir/ Auch meine Zeit beginne . . ." "Der Prinzessin Auguste von Homburg," PF, 110.

65. "Patmos," fragments of the later version, PF, 485.

"Und in der großen Seele, wohlauswählend, den Tod/ Aussprach der Herr, und die letzte Liebe, denn nie genug/ Hatt er, von Güte, zu sagen/ Der Worte, damals, und zu bejahn bejahendes." "Das aber erkannt'er. Alles ist gut. Drauf starb er." "Patmos," PF, 484.

66. "Patmos," PF, 467.

"Denn alles ist gut. Drauf starb er. Vieles wäre/ Zu sagen davon. Und es sah ihn, wie er siegend blikte/ Die Freudigsten die Freunde noch zuletzt." "Patmos," PF, 466.

67. Eckart Förster, *The course of remembrance and other essays on Hölderlin*, edited by Dieter Henrich (Stanford: Stanford Univerity Press, 1997), 221.

68. Ibid., 219.

69. "The Ister," PF, 495.

"Der scheinet aber fast/ Rückwärts zu gehn und/ Ich mein, er müße kommen/ Von Osten./ Vieles wäre/ Zu sagen davon. Und warum hängt er/ An den Bergen gerad?" "Der Ister," PF, 494.

70. David Constantine, *Hölderlin* (Oxford: Clarendon Press, 1988), 47.

71. "Germania," PF, 401.

"Entflohene Götter! auch ihr, ihr gegenwärtigen, damals/ Wahrhaftiger, ihr hattet eure Zeiten!/ Nichts läugnen will ich hier und nichts erbitten." "Germanien," PF, 400.

72. "Celebration of peace," PF, 439.

"Einmal mag aber ein Gott auch Tagewerk erwählen,/ Gleich Sterblichen und theilen alles Schicksaal./ Daß, wenn die Stille kehrt, auch eine Sprache sei." "Friedensfeier," PF, 438.

73. "At the source of the Danube," PF, 385.

"Kommt eine Fremdlingin sie/ Zu uns, die Erwekerin,/ Die menschenbildene Stimme." "Am Quell der Donau," PF, 384.

74. "As on a holiday," PF, 377.

". . . bleibt in den hochherstürzenden Stürmen/ Des Gottes, wenn er nahet,/ das Herz doch fest./ Doch weh mir! wenn von//Weh mir!///Und sag ich gleich//Ich sei genaht, die Himmlischen zu schauen,/ Sie selbst, sie werfen mich tief unter die lebenden,/ Den falschen Priester, ins Dunkel, daß ich/ Das warnende Lied den Gelehrigen singe./ Dort" "Wie wenn am Feiertage . . ." PF, 376.

75. "Voice of the people," second version, PF, 179.

"Das wunderbare Sehnen dem Abgrund zu; / Das Unebundne reizet un Völker auch/ Ergreift die Todelust . . ." "Stimme des Volks," zweite Fassung, PF, 178.

76. "To the fates," PF, 33.

"Einmal/ Lebt ich, wie Götter, und mehr dedarfs nicht." "An die Parzen," PF, 32.

77. Celan, "*The meridian*," PCCP, 50.

"»Aufmerksamkeit«—erlauben Sie mir hier, nach dem Kafka-Essay Walter Benjamins, ein Wort von Malebranche zu zitieren—,»Aufmerksamkeit ist das natürliche Gebet der Seele.«" "Der Meridian," PCDM, 56.

78. Patmos, PF, 477.

". . . der Vater aber liebt,/ Der über allen waltet,/ Am meisten, daß gepfleget werde/ Der veste Buchstab, und bestehendes gut/ Gedeutet." "Patmos," PF, 476.

79. "Germania," PF, 405–07.

"Muß zwischen Tag und Nacht/ Einmals ein Wahres erscheinen./ Dreifach umschreibe du es,/ Doch ungesprochen auch, wie es da ist,/ Unschuldige, muß er bleiben." "Germanien," PF, 404–06. (*Virgin* is in fact the translator's addition, most probably to give us the sense that *Unschuldige*, "innocent," is nominative.)

80. "Duino Elegies," First Elegy, in *The selected poetry of Rainer Maria Rilke*, bilingual edition, edited and translated by Stephen Mitchell (NY: Vintage Books, 1989), 151. Hereafter, SPRMR.

"Wer, wenn ich schreie, hörte mich denn aus der Engel/ Ordungen?" Erste Elegie, SPRMR, 150.

81. "The notebooks of Malte Laurids Brigge," SPRMR, 113.

". . . begriff sein an Fernen gewohntes Gefühl Gottes äussersten Abstand. Nächte kamen, da er meinte, sich auf ihn zuzuwerfen in den Raum; Stunden voller Entdeckung, in denen er sich stark genug fühlte, nach der Erde zu tauchen, um sie hinaufzureissen auf der Sturmflut seines Herzens. Er war wie einer, der eine herrliche Sprache hört und fiebernd sich vornimmt, in ihr zu dichten. Noch stand ihm die Bestürzung bevor, zu erfahren, wie schwer diese Sprache sei . . ." SPRMR, 112.

82. SPRMR, 91.

"Und es genügt auch noch nicht, daß man Erinnerungen hat. Man muß sie vergessen können, wenn es viele sind, und man muss die große Geduld haben, zu warten, dass sie wiederkommen." SPRMR, 90.

83. "Buddha," SPRMR, 49.

"Als ob er horchte. Stille: eine Ferne . . . / Wir halten ein und hören sie nicht mehr." "Buddha," SPRMR, 48.

84. "Duino Elegies," First Elegy, SPRMR, 153.

"Höre, mein Herz, wie sonst nur/ Heilige hörten: daß sie der riesige Ruf/ aufhob vom Boden; sie aber knieten,/ Unmögliche, weiter, und achtetens nicht:/ So waren sie hörend. Nicht daß du Gottes ertrügest/ die Stimme, bei weitem. Aber das Wehende höre,/ die ununterbrochene Nachricht, die aus Stille sich bildet." "Duino Elegien," Erste Elegie, SPRMR, 48.

85. Niebylski, op.cit., 118.

86. "Funeral monument of a young girl," in *Rainer Maria Rilke: New poems [1907]*, bilingual edition, translated by Edward Snow (NY: Farrar, Strauss and Giroux, 1984), 17.

"Wir gendenkens noch. Das ist, als müßte/ alles dieses einmal wieder sein." *New poems*, 16.

87. "Requiem," SPRMR, 83.

"Ich möchte meine Stimme wie ein Tuch/ hinwerfen über deines Todes Scherben/ und zerrn an ihr, bis sie in Fetzen geht,/ und alles, was ich sage, müßte so/ zerlumpt in dieser Stimme gehn und frieren;/ blieb es beim Klagen." "Requiem," SPRMR, 82.

88. "You who never arrived," SPRMR, 131.

"Du im Voraus/ verlorne Geliebte, nimmergekommene,/ nicht weiß ich, welche Töne dir leib sind." SPRMR, 130.

89. "Requiem," SPRMR, 73.

"Daß wir erschranken, da du starbst, nein, daß/ dein starker Tod uns dunkel unterbrach,/ das Bisdahin abreissend vom Seither . . ." "Requiem," SPRMR, 72.

90. "Duino elegies," First Elegy, SPRMR, 155.

". . . Seltsam,/ alles, was sich bezog, so lose im Raume/ flattern zu sehen. Und das Totsein is mühsam/ und voller Nachholn, daß man all mählich ein wening/ Ewigkeit Spürt.—Aber Lebendiger machen/ alle den Fehler, daß sie zu stark unterscheiden." Erste Elegie, SPRMR, 154.

91. "Duino elegies," Fourth Elegy, SPRMR, 173.

"Aber dies: den Tod,/ den ganzen Tod, noch vor dem Leben so/ sanft zu enthalten und nicht bös zu sein,/ ist unbeschreiblich." Vierte Elegie, SPRMR, 172.

92. "Duino elegies," Ninth Elegy, SPRMR, 203.

"Siehe, ich lebe. Woraus? Weder Kindheit noch Zukunft/ werden weniger," Neunte Elegie, SPRMR, 202.

93. Ninth Elegy, SPRMR, 199–201.

"Sind wir vielleicht hier, um zu sagen: Haus,/ Brücke, Brunnen, Tor, Krug, Obstbaum, Fenster,—/ höchstens, Säule, Turm . . . aber zu *sagen*, verstehs,/ oh zu sagen *so*, wie selber die Dinge niemals/ innig meinten zu sagen." "Preise dem Engel die Welt." Neunte Elegie, SPRMR, 198–200.

94. "Duino elegies," Fourth Elegy, SPRMR,195.

". . . was uns/ oft überwältigt,—die Erinnerung,/ als sei schon einmal das, wonach man drängt/ näher gewesen, treuer und sein Anschluß/ unendlich ärtlich. Hier ist alles Abstand,/ und dort wars Atem. Nach der ersten Heimat/ ist ihm die zwiete Zwitterig und windig." Vierte Elegie, SPRMR, 194

95. Celan, "I make you at home,/ instead of all/ rest." "Do not work ahead," PPC, 315.

"nehm ich dich auf,/ statt aller/ Ruhe." "Wirk nicht voraus," PPC, 314.

96. Ninth Elegy, SPRMR, 199.

"Aber weil Hiersein viel ist, und weil uns scheinbar/ alles das Hiesige braucht, dieses Schwindenden, das/ seltsam uns angeht. Uns, die Schwindensten./. . . Und wir auch/ *ein* Mal. Nie wieder. Aber dieses/ *ein* Mal gewesen zu sein, wenn auch nur ein Mal:/ *irdisch* gewesen zu sein, scheint nicht widerrufbar." Neunte Elegie, SPRMR, 198. (Though Rilke does have an ecological sense to which I cannot do justice here, the translation may overstate this; "irdisch gewesen zu sein" suggests to be essentially earthly.)

97. Eighth Elegy, SPRMR, 197.

"Who has twisted us around like this, so that/ no matter what we do, we are in the posture/ of someone going away?"

"Wer hat uns also umgedreht, daß wir,/ was wir auch tun, in jener Haltung sind/ von einem, welcher fortgeht?" Achte Elegie, SPRMR, 196.

98. See Hans Egon Holthusen, *Rainer Maria Rilke: a study of his later poetry*, translated by J. P. Stern (New Haven: Yale, 1952), 24. "Feeling is endless remembrance, intensification [his note: The German for 'a memory,' *Erinnerung*, has just this connotation of inwardness and emotional intensity] re-presentation and realisation; hence it is the enemy of time, and of itself creative of space."

99. "Requiem" SPRMR 81.

"aber/ nun warst du in der Zeit, und Zeit ist lang./ Und Zeit geht hin, und Zeit nimmt zu . . ." "Requiem," SPRMR 81.

chapter four

1. We should note, though, that not all readers and critics agree that this was Augustine's intent. Margaret Miles suggests that for Augustine erotic pleasure was so overwhelming as to have an addictive quality; his celibacy was his solution to his own desire rather than a prescription for all of humanity. See "Desire and Delight," in *Broken and whole*, edited by Maureen Tilley and Susan Ross (Lanham, MD: University Press of America, 1995).

2. Mackey, 8.

3. Ibid., 7.

4. See St. Augustine, *Confessions*, translated by Henry Chadwick (NY: Oxford University Press, 1991), X.xi (18), X.xvii (26), et cetera. In Plato, see especially the *Meno*, 82A–86C, in *The collected dialogues of Plato*.

5. *Confessions*, X.i/1.

6. Cf. Mackey, "Book 10, usually taken to be Augustine's 'theory of memory,' consists almost entirely of unanswered questions that turn into prayers for healing and enlightenment. Augustine desires a perfect knowledge of God. What he gets is a deeper and more troubled awareness of his own predicament." Mackey, 39.

7. Cf. Turner, 58.

8. Turner, 66. Cf. Mackey: "Always a wanderer and never (save in hope) at rest by the hearth, always burning but never consumed, Augustine circles the central fire forever in questioning and in prayer." Mackey, 44.

9. *Confessions*, XI.i/1.

"iam dixi et dicam: amore amoris tui facio istuc." "ecce narravi tibi multa, quae potui et quae volui, quoniam tu prior voluisti, ut confiterer tibi, domino deo meo . . ." in *St. Augustine's Confessions, with an English translation by William Watts* (NY: G. P. Putnam's Sons, 1931), XI.i. Chadwick's translation and the Putnam edition are the sources of all further citations from the *Confessions* unless otherwise noted.

10. Ibid., X.iii/3.

"sed credunt mihi, quorum mihi aures caritas aperit."

11. Ibid., X.iii/4.

"dicit enim eis caritas, qua boni sunt, non mentiri me de me confitentem, et ipsa in eis credit mihi."

12. Mackey, 11.

13. *Confessions*, XI.xiii/15.

"cum ergo sis operator omnium temporum, si fuit aliquod tempus . . . id ipsum enim tempus tu feceras . . ."

14. Ibid., XI.xiv/17.

"quid est ergo tempus? si nemo ex me quaerat, scio; si quaerenti explicare velim, nescio . . ."

15. Ibid., XI.xv/20.

"et ipsa una hora fugitivis particulis agitur: quidquid eius avolavit, praeteritum est, quidquid ei restat, futurum. si quid intellegitur temporis, quod in nullas iam vel minutissimas momentorum partes dividi possit, id solum est, quod praesens dicatur; quod tamen ita raptim a futuro in praeteritum transvolat, ut nulla morula extendatur.nam si extenditur, dividitur in praeteritum et futurum: praesens autem nullum habet spatium."

16. Ibid., XI.xxi/27.

". . . metimur, nec metiri quae non sunt possumus, et non sunt praeterita vel futura. praesens vero tempus quomodo metimur, quando non habet spatium?"

17. Ibid., XI.xiv/17.

"duo ergo illa tempora, praeteritum et futurum, quomodo sunt, quando et praeteritum iam non est et futurum nondum est? praesens autem si semper esset praesens nec in praeteritum transiret, . . . si ergo praesens, ut tempus sit, ideo fit, quia in praeteritum transit, quomodo et hoc esse dicimus, cui causa, ut sit, illa est, quia non erit, ut scilicet non vere dicamus tempus esse, nisi quia tendit non esse?"

18. Ibid., X.viii/14.

". . . et cum dico, praesto sunt imagines omnium quae dico ex eodem thesauro memoriae, nec omnino aliquid eorum dicerem, si defuissent."

19. Ibid., XI.xvii/22.

"nam ubi ea viderunt qui futura cecinerunt, si nondum sunt? neque enim potest videri id quod non est. et qui narrant praeterita, non utique vera narrarent, si animo illa non cernerent: quae si nulla essent, cerni omnino non possent. sunt ergo et futura et praeterita."

20. Ibid., XI.xx/26.

"Quod autem nunc liquet et claret,nec futura sunt nec praeterita, nec proprie dicitur: tempora sunt tria, praeteritum, praesens et futurum, sed fortasse proprie diceretur: tempora sunt tria, praesens de praetcritis, praesens de praesentibus, praesens de futuris."

21. Ibid.

"sunt enim haec in anima tria quaedam, et alibi ea non video."

22. Ibid., XI.xxvii/340.

"et metimur tamen tempora, nec ea, quae nondum sunt, nec ea, quae iam non sunt, nec ea, quae nulla mora extenduntur, nec ea, quae terminos non habent. nec futura ergo nec praeterita nec praesentia nec praetereuntia tempora metimur, et metimur tamen tempora."

23. Ibid., XI.xxvi/33.

"an tempore breviore metimur longius . . . ? sic enim videmus spatio brevis syllabae metiri spatium longae syllabae atque id duplum dicere."

24. Ibid.

"distentionem . . . ipsius animi."

25. Ibid., X.vi/8, X.vi/9, X.vi/10, XI.iv/6.

26. Ibid., X.viii/13.

27. Ibid., XI.ii/3, X.ii/2.

28. Ibid., X.xxvi/37, XI.ii/4, XI.iii/5, XI.xxvii/34.

29. Ibid., X.viii/14.

30. Ibid., X.xxxv/54.

"neque enim dicimus: audi quid rutilet, aut: olefac quam niteat, aut: gusta quam splendeat, aut: palpa quam fulgeat: videri enim dicuntur haec omnia. dicimus autem non solum: vide quid lucet, quod soli oculi sentire possunt, sed etiam: vide quid sonet, vide quid oleat, vide quid sapiat, vide quam durum sit."

31. Compare *The teacher*, chapter 4: "Thus it is that when a word is written a sign is presented to the eyes, and this brings into the mind what pertains to hearing." in St. Augustine: *The greatness of the soul and The teacher*, translated by Joseph M. Colleran, (Westminster, MD: The Newman Press, 1950).

32. *Confessions*, X.ii/2.

"neque id ago verbis carnis et vocibus, sed verbis animae et clamore cogitationis . . . confessio itaque mea, deus meus, in conspectu tuo tibi tacite fit et non tacite. tacet enim strepitu, clamat affectu."

33. Ibid., XI.xxvii/34.

"adtende . . . ecce puta vox corporis incipit sonare et sonat et adhuc sonat et ecce desinit, iamque silentium est . . ."

34. Ibid., XI.vi/8, ref. Matt 17:5: "Hic est filius meus dilectus."

35. Ibid., XI.vii/9.

". . . quod sempiterne dicitur et eo sempiterne dicuntur omnia . . . et ideo verbo tibi coaeterno simul et sempiterne dicis omnia, quae dicis, et fit, quidquid dicis ut fiat . . ."

36. Ibid., XI.xxvii/35.

"aliquid in memoria mea metior, quod infixum manet."

37. Turner, 69.

38. Ibid., X.xvi/24.

"memoria retinetur oblivio."

39. Ibid., X.xvi/25.

". . . inexplicabilis, ipsam oblivionem meminisse me certus sum, qua id quod meminerimus obruitur."

40. Ibid., X.xxv/36.

"habitas certe in ea, quoniam tui memini, ex quo te didici, et in ea invenio, cum recordor te."

Cf. Turner: "A more general, conceptual question which will preoccupy Augustine throughout this work, but especially in Book 10: how can we be said to be searching for something if we do not know what we are searching for; and how, by contrast, if we do know what we are searching for, can we be said to be *searching* for it at all." Turner, 57.

41. *Confessions*, X.xxvi/37.

42. Ibid., X.viii/12.

"campos et lata praetoria memoriae . . ."

43. Ibid., X.x/17.

"ubi ergo, aut quare, cum dicerentur, agnovi et dixi: 'ita est, verum est,' nisi quia iam erant in memoria . . ."

Cf. *Meno*. 85c–86b.

44. *Confessions*, XI.xxix/39.

"pater meus aeternus es; at ego in tempora dissilui, quorum ordinem nescio, et tumultuosis varietatibus dilaniantur cogitationes meae, intima viscera animae meae . . ."

45. Ibid.

"donec in te confluam purgatus et liquidus igne amoris tui."

46. Ibid., XI.xxxi/4.1

"ita tibi aliquid accidit inconmutabiliter aeterno, hoc est vere aeterno creatori mentium."

"expectiatione vocum futurarum et memoria praeteritarum variatur affectus sensuque distenditur . . ."

chapter five

1. Occasionally, however, Augustine does prove unexpectedly generous in this regard, as in Book XII of the *Confessions*: "So what difficulty is it for me when these words [of Genesis] can be interpreted in various ways, provided only that the interpretations are true? What difficulty is it for me, I say, if I understand the text in a way

different from someone else, who understands the scriptural author in another sense? In Bible study all of us are trying to find and grasp the meaning of the author we are reading. . . . As long as each interpreter is endeavoring to find in the holy scriptures the meaning of the author who wrote it, what evil is it if an exegesis he gives is one shown to be true by you, light of all sincere souls, even if the author whom he is reading did not have that idea and, though he had grasped at truth, had not discerned that seen by the interpreter?" *Confessions*, XII.xviii (27).

"quae mihi ardenter confitenti, deus meus, lumen oculorum meorum in occulto, quid mihi obest, cum diversa in his verbis intellegi possint, quae tamen vera sint? quid, inquam, mihi obest, si aliud ego sensero, quam sensit alius eum sensisse, qui scripsit? omnes quidem, qui legimus, nitimur hoc indagare atque conprehendere . . . dum ergo quisque conatur id sentire in scripturis sanctis, quod in eis sensit ille qui scripsit, quid mali est, si hoc sentiat, quod tu, lux omnium veridicarum mentium, ostendis verum esse, etiamsi non hoc sensit ille, quem legit, cum et ille verum nec tamen hoc senserit?"

In fact, the Augustine of the *Confessions*, the work with which I have been concerned here, seems in general more open-minded, perhaps because more open-ended, in his discussion than Augustine does elsewhere. This is perhaps because of the personal and exploratory nature of the *Confessions*, a work devoted to questions as much as to answers.

2. In fact, a minority faction is even pushing for canonization (Bruce Milem, personal communication, 1998).

3. The category of "mystic" is in any case a problematic one, but certainly if mysticism is experientially-based religion then Eckhart does not fit it. As Turner rightly points out, "Eckhart no more argues from experience than he argues to experience, his own or anyone else's." Turner, 174.

4. Meister Eckhart, "Selections from Eckhart's defense," in *Meister Eckhart: the essential sermons, commentaries, treatises, and defence*, translated and introduced by Edmund Colledge and Bernard McGinn (NY: Paulist Press, 1981), 72.

5. Meister Eckhart, sermon 83, in *Meister Eckhart: selected writings*, translated by Oliver Davies (NY: Penguin Books, 1994), 236. Hereafter, SW.

"Sprich ich nv̇: ,got ist gv̂t'—Es ist nit war, mer: Ich bin gût, got ist nit gût! Ich wil me sprechen: ,Ich bin besser danne got!' wan swaz gût ist, das mag bessir werden; was besser mag werden, das mag aller best werden." *Meister Eckhart: Die deutschen und lateinischen Werke*, dritter Band (Stuttgart: W. Kohlhammer, 1976), 441. Hereafter, DLW.

6. Sells, 177.

7. John Caputo, *The prayers and tears of Jacques Derrida: Religion without religion* (Bloomington: Indiana University Press, 1997), 10.

8. Ibid., 11.

9. Meister Eckhart, commentary on St. John's gospel, "In the beginning was the Word, and the Word was with God, and the Word was God," in *The best of Meister*

Eckhart, edited by Halcyon Backhouse (NY: Crossroad Publishing, 1992), 109. Hereafter, BME.

10. Sermon 50, SW, 136–37.

"Das erste: das gv̂t, das si bekanten vnd sahen in gotte, das was so gros vnd so verborgen, das es sich nicht erbilden mochte in irme verstantnisse; want alles, das sich erbilden mochte, das was dem als vngelich, das si sahen in gotte, vnd was so valsch wider der warheit, das si swigen vnd wolten nicht liegen.—Dv̇ ander sache: alles, das si in gotte sachen, das was so gelich gros vnd edele, das si weder bilde noch forme moechten da von genemen ze redende.—Dv̇ dritte sache, war vmbe sid verstumeten, das was, das sie sahen in dei verborgenen warheit vnd fvnden die heimlicheit kerten vnd da sprachen; vnd vond der vungelicheit der warheit do vielen si in die groben materie vnd wolten vns leren got bekennen mit den nideren dingen der creature." DLW, II, 1971, 454.

11. Amy Hollywood, *The soul as virgin wife: Mechthild of Magdeburg, Marguerite Porete, and Meister Eckhart* (Notre Dame: University of Notre Dame Press, 1995), 149.

12. Cf. Turner: "For Eckhart, 'my' self is in the last resort not *mine* at all. And any self which I can call my own self is a false self, a self of possessive imagination." Turner, 184.

13. See *Thought from the outside*, 9f.

14. In *Meister Eckhart: Image and Discourse in Four German Sermons*, Milem argues that "Eckhart . . . primarily involves his audience in a complex interpretive exercise by deliberately giving difficult sermons that emphasize their own status as products of language. The sermons' self-referential quality opens the door to thinking about the relation between the sermons and the divine truths they claim to articulate." (forthcoming, Catholic University Press), 1. Later Milem remarks, "Eckhart's use of language disrupts any expectation of ordinary, matter-of-fact speech and raises a number of questions about what is happening in the sermon." 9.

15. Sermon 52, SW 204.

"Dô ich stuont in mîner êrsten sache, dô enhâte ich keinen got, und dô was ich sache mîn selbes; dô enwolte ich niht, noch enbegerte ich niht, . . . Dô wolte ich mich selben und enwolte kein ander dinc; daz ich wolte, daz was ich, und daz ich was, daz wolte ich, und hie stuont ich ledic gotes und aller dinge. Aber dô ich ûzgienc von mînem vrîen willen und ich enpfienc mîn geschaffen wesen, dô hâte ich einen got . . ." DLW, zweiter Band, 492.

16. "Commentary on St. John's gospel," BME 109.

17. Sermon 39, SW 147.

"Ez sprichet ein geschrift: 'vor der gemacheten werlt bin ich'. Er sprichet: 'vor' 'bin ich', daz ist: dâ der mensche erhaben ist über zît in êwicheit, dâ würket der mensche ein werk mit gote." DLW, II, 261.

18. Hollywood, 189.

19. Aristotle, *Metaphysics*, translated by Richard Hope (NY: Columbia Univesity Press, 1952), Book Lambda, 7.1027a, approximately 22–25.

20. Ibid., 1027a, approximately 25–27.

21. Ibid., 1027b, approximately 12–13.

22. See St. Thomas Aquinas, *Summa Theologiae*, translated by the Fathers of the English Dominican Province (NY: Benzinger Brothers, 1925) I, 2, 3: Whether God exists?

23. Plotinus, *Enneads*, translated by Stephen Mackenna (NY: Penguin Books, 1991), V.II, "The origin and order of the beings following on the first," sec. 1.

24. Sells, 8.

25. Eckhart, "Where is the one who is born the king of the Jews" (Matt. 2:2), BME 18. This sermon does not appear to be in the DLW.

26. See Augustine, *Confessions*, III.vii (12).

27. Personal communication from Peter Manchester, 1998. Cited from the *Exsultet* for the Easter Vigil, from the Latin Sacramentary. I am deeply indebted to Peter Manchester for the source and exact form of this quotation.

28. Sermon 38, SW, 117.

"Dâ von ist got got, daz er âne crêatûre ist. Er ennante sich niht in der zît. In der zît ist crêatûre und sünde und tôt." DLW, II, 241.

29. Sermon 83, SW, 236–37.

"do von swig vnd klafe nit von gotte; wande mit dem, so dv̇ von ime claffest, so lv̇gest dv̇, so tv̇stu svnde. wiltu nv̇ ane svnde sin vnd vollekomen, so claffe nit von gotte." DLW, III Band, 442.

30. Sermon 38, SW, 115.

"Diu sêle enhât ouch keinen namen; als wênic als man gote eigenen namen vinden mac, als wênic mac man der sêle eigenen namen vinden, aleine dâ grôziu buoch von geschriben sîn. Aber dâ si ein ûzluogen hât ze den werken, dâ von gibet man ir namen." DLW, II, 237.

31. Sermon 36a, BME, 62. "Ich spriche, daz got sî ungesprochen. Nû sprichet sant Augustînus, daz got ensî niht ungesprochen; wan waere er ungesprochen, daz selbe waere ein spruch, wan er ist mê ein swîgen dan ein sprechen." DLW, II, 189.

32. Ibid., 63.

"Nû sprechen wir, daz got ein geist ist. Des enist niht. Waere got eigenlîche ein geist, sô waere er gesprochen. Sant Grêgôrius sprichet: wir enmügen von gote niht eigenlîche sprechen. Waz wir von im sprechen, daz müezen wir stameln." DLW, II, 190–91.

33. Sermon 30, SW, 124.

". . . got ensprach nie dan einez. Sîn spruch enist niht dan einez. In dem éinen spruche sprichet er sînen sun und den heiligen geist mite und alle crêatûren und enist niht dan éin spruch in gote." DLW, II, 98.

34. Sermon 1, SW, 156.

"Sol aber Jêsus reden in der sêle, sô muoz si aleine sîn und muoz selber swîgen, sol si Jêsum hoeren reden. . . . Waz sprichet her Jêsus? Er sprichet, daz er ist. Waz ist er denne? Er ist ein wort des vaters." DLW, I, 15.

35. Ibid., 157.

"Und daz selbe wort, als ez in im selber ist, diz hât der vater allez gesprochen, daz wort und allez, daz in dem worte ist." DLW, I, 16.

36. "Where is the one who is born the king of the Jews?" BME, 17.

37. "According to one authority, the sense of hearing is much nobler than the sense of sight. For we learn wisdom more through the ear than the eye. . . . Hearing draws in more, seeing leads out more. . . . Hearing, I am receptive; seeing, I am active." "Where is the one who is born the king of the Jews?" BME, 18.

38. "I must be about my father's business." BME, 31.This, too, does not appear to be in DLW.

39. Unnamed sermon, SW, 246.

"Aber do si ein sein in dem wesen, da ensein si niht geleich, wann geleicheit stet in underscheid. Also sprich ich von der sele: sol si kûmen in die gotlichen einikeit, so mûz si die geleicheit verliesen, di si hat in dem ewigen bild. . . . Ein heidnisch meister spricht: Got ist, dez niht erfullet alleu dink, und sein iht ist niendert. Dor um gotes iht daz enwirt niht fûnden von der sele, ez sei denn, daz si sey zu niht worden . . ." in F. Jostes, ed., *Meister Eckhart und seine Jünger: ungedruckte zur Geschichte der deutschen Mystik* (De Gruyter, 1972), 94.

40. Ibid, 247.

"Diz ist der ander tot und der ander auzgank, da di sele get auz irem wesen, daz si hat in dem ewigen bild, zu sûchen daz reich gots." Jostes, 95.

41. Sermon 38, SW, 113.

"Alsô wirt daz êwige wort gesprochen inwendic in dem herzen der sêle, in dem innersten, in dem lûtersten, in dem houbete der sêle, . . . in vernünfticheit: dâ geschihet diu geburt inne." DLW, II, 229–30.

42. Sermon 52, SW, 204. See note 10.

43. Turner, 182.

44. "I must be about my Father's business," BME, 24.

45. "St. James says in his epistle . . ." BME, 66. Does not appear to be in DLW.

46. W 56, DP 26, SW, 233. Not in DLW.

47. Sermon 83, SW, 238–39.

"Dv̇ solt [got] minnen, als er ist Ein nit-got, Ein nit-geist, Ein nit-persone, Ein nu̇t-bilde, Mer: als er ein luter pur clar Ein ist, gesvndert von aller zweiheite, vnd in dem einen sv̇len wir ewiklich versinken von nite zv̇ nv̇te. Dis helf vns got. amen." DLW, III, 448.

48. Ibid., 237.

"Dv solt alzemal entzinken diner dinisheit vnd solt zer fliesen in sine sinesheit vnd sol din din *vnd* sin *sin* éin min werden als genzlich, das dv̇ mit ime verstandest ewiklich sin vngewordene istikeit vnd sin vngenanten nitheit." DLW, III, 443.

49. Ibid., 238.

"Got mv̊s vil bi ich werden vnd ich vil bi got, alse gar ein, das dis ‚er' vnd dis ‚ich' Ein ‚ist' werdent . . . Ein einig ‚hie' oder ein einig ‚nv̊', so mochte dis ‚ich' mit dem ‚er' niemer gewirken noch ein gewerden." DLW, III, 447.

50. J82, SW, 244.

". . . ich sprich: dez ist mer not in sulcher weis, volkûmen zu werden, daz di sele got verliese denn sie verliez di creatur. . . . Dizz ist alles di meinung gotes, daz di sele got verlies; wann als lang als di sele got hat und got bekent und got weiz, so ist si verre von got. Daz ist gots begerung, daz got sich selber zu nicht mach in der sele, uf daz die sele sich selber verliese. Wann daz got got heizt, daz hat er von den creaturen. Do di sele creatur wart, do het si einen got; als di sele geschaffenheit verleuset, so beleibt got im selber, daz er ist; und daz ist di meist ere, di die sele got tût, daz ist, daz si got im selber lazze und ste (si) sein ledik." Jostes 93.

chapter six

1. Levinas, PN, 4, see n2.

"L'inquiétude nouvelle, du langage-en-dérive, n'annonce-t-elle pas, sans périphrases . . . , la fin du monde?

Le temps ne transmet plus son sens dans la simultanéité des phrases. Les propositions n'arrivent plus à mettre ensemble les choses. . . . Comme si l'anamnèse platonicienne qui maintenait pendant des siècles l'unité de la Représentation, se faisait amnésie et comme si le désordre ne s'assemblait pas forcément en un ordre autre." *Noms propres* (Paris: Fata Morgana, 1976), 10. Hereafter, NP.

2. Hill, MBEC, 173.

3. Hill, MBEC, 175.

4. Jacques Derrida, "Sauf le nom," in *On the name*, edited Thomas Dutoit (Stanford: Stanford University Press, 1995), 58. Hereafter, SN. Ellipsis in original.

"Mais perdre le nom, ce n'est pas s'en prendre à lui, le détruire ou le blesser. Au contraire, c'est tout simplement le respecter: comme nom. C'est-à-dire le prononcer, ce qui revient à le traverser vers l'autre, qu'il nomme et qui le porte. Le prononcer sans le prononcer. L'oublier en l'appelant, en (se) le rappelant, ce qui revient à appeler ou se rappeler l'autre. . . ." *Sauf le nom* (Paris: Éditions Galilée, 1993), 61. Hereafter, SlN.

5. SN, 68.

"Et comme en toute signature humaine ou divine, il y faut le nom. A moins que . . . le nom ne soit ce qui s'efface devant ce qu'il nomme, et alors «il faut le nom» voudrait dire que le nom fait défaut: il doit faire défaut, il faut un nom qui fasse défaut." SlN, 79–80.

6. Cf. Derrida: "—Yes, but the *Confessions* themselves were already, in their wildest present, in their date, in their place, an act of memory." SN, 40.

"—Oui, mais elles-mêmes étaient déjà, dans leur présent le plus sauvage, à leur date, en leur lieu, un acte de mémoire." SIN, 26. The context makes clear that the *Confessions* is the work under discussion.

7. IC 50.

"Laissons Dieu de côté, nom trop imposant." EI 71. Cited in Hill, MBEC, 173.

8. Hölderlin, "Patmos," PF, 463.

"Nah is/ Und schwer zu fassen der Gott." "Patmos," PF, 462.

9. Augustine writes, "Where then did I find you in order to be able to learn of you? . . . There is no place, whether we go backwards or forwards; there can be no question of place." *Confessions* X.xxvi.

"Ubi ergo te inveni, ut discerem te? . . . et nusquam locus, et recedimus et accedimus, et nusquam locus."

10. Blanchot, *Friendship*, translated by Elizabeth Rottenberg (Stanford: Stanford University Press, 1997), 236.

"Ce sera la part d'Isaac Luria. . . . On pourrait croire que la pensée de l'exil . . . va trancher définitivement les plans divin et terrestre et livrer l'homme à l'attente impuissante. Mais l'exil ne peut pas être un événement seulement local . . . il est aussi l'exil de Dieu, la séparation d'une part de Dieu avec lui-même, la souffrance des parcelles de lumières maintenues captives dans l'obscurité. On reconnaît à l'antique conception de la gnose . . . c'est la Sophia, la lumière tombée dans les ténèbres, un être abondonné et cependant divin, séparé de son origine, et cependant non séparé, car la séparation s'appelle temps, et la réunion éternité. Dans la plupart des doctrines gnostiques, c'est par le ciel seul que peut être rappelée l'âme divine, tombée sur la terre: il n'y a qu'une action possible, celle qui est dirigée du haut vers le bas. Mais, note Buber, dans la pensée mystique juive, fondée sur un rapport de réciprocité, sur un dialogue libre entre le moi terrestre et le Toi divin, l'homme reste l'auxiliaire de Dieu. Les sphères sont séparées pour que l'homme les rapproche. Toute la création et Dieu même sont dans l'attent de l'homme." *L'Amitié*, (Paris: Gallimard, 1971), 268.

11. "Come, come, come, you whom the injunction, the prayer, the wait could not suit." SNB, 135.

"Viens, viens, venez, vous auquel ne saurait convenir l'injonction, la prière, l'attente." PAD, 185.

12. Sermon 52, SW, 207.

"Her umbe sô bite ich got, daz er mich ledic mache gotes . . ." DLW, zweiter Band, 502.

13. See *Holy Bible: New International Version*, Matthew 27: 46–47 and Mark 15: 34–35.

14. Ludwig Wittgenstein, "Ethics, life and faith," in *The Wittgenstein reader*, edited by Anthony Kenny, Cambridge: Blackwell, 1994, 297. I am indebted to Alexander Caswell for bringing this passage to my attention.

15. PN, 137.

"L'espace littéraire où nous conduit Blanchot . . . n'a rien de commun avec le monde heideggerien que l'art rend habitable. L'art, d'après Blanchot, loin d'éclairer le monde, laisse apercevior le sous-sol désolé, fermé à toute lumière qui le sous-tend et rend à notre séjour son essence d'exil et aux merveilles de notre architecture—leur fonction de cabanes dans le désert. Pour Blanchot, comme pour Heidegger, l'art ne conduit pas . . . vers un monde derrière le monde réel. Il est lumière. Lumière d'en-haut pour Heidegger, faisant le monde, fondant le lieu. Noire lumière pour Blanchot, nuit venant d'en-bas, lumière qui défait le monde, le ramenant à son origine, au ressassement, au murmure, au clapotement incessant, à un «profond jadis, jadis jamais assez».

. . . Il ne s'agit pas de revenir en arrière. Mais pour Blanchot, la littérature rappelle l'essence humaine du nomadisme. Le nomadisme n'est-il pas la source d'un sens, apparaissant dans une lumière que ne renvoie aucun marbre, mais le visage de l'homme." SMB, 24.

16. *Friendship*, 217–18.

"Ce rapport est celui d'une distance. Cette distance est absolue. A cette distance absolue, ce qui surgit devant nous, mais comme sans nous, est le «surgissement d'une présence»; la présence n'est pas quelque chose de présent; ce qui est là, non pas s'approchant, non pas se dérobant, ignorant tous les jeux de l'insaisissable, est là avec l'évidence abrupte de la présence, laquelle refuse le graduel, le progressif, le lent avènement, l'insensible disparition et cependant désigne une relation infinie. La présence est le surgissement de la «présence séparée»: cela qui vient à nous hors de pair, immobile dans la soudaineté de la venue et s'offrant étranger, tel quel en son étrangeté." *L'Amitié*, 246–47.

17. PN, 131.

"Etre, équivaut à parler, mais parler en absence de tout interlocuteur." SMB 15.

18. Jabès, TBR, vol. 3, 31.

"Il ne s'agit point de se retrancher derrière l'impossibilité d'écrire que cette impossibilité; mais, au contraire, de repousser jusqu'à l'impossibilité cette possibilité illusoire; car rien ne s'écrit qui ne fut déjà maintes fois récit." LR, 320.

19. Levinas, PN, 145 and 146. Notes cite quotations from Blanchot, *L'attente l'oubli*, 17 and 45.

"Elle luttait, dit Blanchot, «contre certains mots qui avaient été comme déposés en elle et qu'elle s'efforçait de maintenir en rapport avec l'avenir ou avec quelque chose qui ne s'était pas encore passé, tout de même déjà présent, tout de même déjà passé». C'est peut-être ce mouvement qui défait les mots réduits au présent que Blanchot nomme l'Attente, l'Oubli." SMB, 36. "Là encore l'Oubli restitue la diachronie

au temps. Diachronie sans protention, ni rétention. Ne rien attendre et tout oublier—
le contraire de la subjectivité—«absence de tout centre». Décontraction de Moi—de
sa tension sure soi . . ." SMB, 37

20. WD, 76.

"L'oubli est une pratique, la pratique d'une écriture qui prophétise parce qu'elle
s'accomplit en renonçant à tout: annoncer, c'est renoncer peut-être." ED, 122.

21. NVC, 56.

"un brusque réveil . . ." NCV 93.

22. Foucault, *Thought from the outside* , 24.

"chambre plus longue que large, éroite comme un tunnel, où distance et l'approche,—l'approche de l'oubli, la distance de l'attente—se rapprochent l'un de l'autre
et indéfinement s'éloignent." "Le pensée du dehors," 529.

23. Blanchot, *Celui qui ne m'accompagnait pas* (Paris: Gallimard, 1953), 125–26.
Cited and translated in Foucault, *Thought from the outside* , 22–23.

". . . nonpas une parole, à peine un murmure, à peine un frisson, moins que le
silence, moins que l'abîme du vide: la plénitude du vide, quelque chose qu'on ne peut
faire taire, occupant tout l'espace, l'ininterrompu et l'incessant, un frisson et déjà un
murmure, non pas un murmure, mais une parole, et non pas une parole quelconque,
mais distincte, juste: à ma portée." (See reference above.)

24. LBUS, 58.

". . . silence qui a oublié." PLSHS, 64.

25. Ibid., 75.

"«Écrire, disait-il, est un acte de silence dirigé contre le silence; le premier acte
positif de la mort cotre la mort.»" 81.

26. Arkady Plotnitsky, "The Maze of Taste: On Bataille, Derrida, and Kant," in
OBCE, 124.

27. Lionel Abel, "Georges Bataille and the repetition of Nietzsche," OBCE, 57.
Original not fully cited.

28. Maurice Blanchot, *Awaiting oblivion*, translated John Gregg (Lincoln: University of Nebraska Press, 1997), 3.

"Ce qu'elle dit, les secrets que tu recueilles et que tu transcris pour les faire val-
oir, tu dois les ramener doucement, malgré leur tentative de séduction, vers le silence
que tu as d'abord puisé en eux." *L'attente l'oubli* (Paris: Gallimard, 1962), 11.

29. Ninth Elegy, SPRMR 199.

". . . Haus,/ Brücke, Brunnen, Tor, Krug, Obstbaum, Fenster,—/ höchstens, Säule,
Turm . . ." Neunte Elegie, SPRMR, 198. A few lines later, as I have noted, Rilke adds:

"Praise this world to the angel, not the unsayable one,/. . ./ Tell him of Things.
He will stand astonished." SPRMR, 201.

"Preise dem Engel die Welt, nicht die unsägliche,/. . ./ Sag ihm die Dinge. Er wird
staunender stehn." SPRMR, 200.

30. Eliot, "The Dry Salvages," V, in *Four Quartets*. "Men's curiosity searches past and future/ And clings to that dimension. But to apprehend/ The point of intersection of the timeless/ With time, is an occupation for the saint—/No occupation either, but something given/ And taken, in a lifetime's death in love. . . ."

31. "Burnt Norton," I, in *Four Quartets*.

32. *Confessions* , II.i.1.

"amore amoris tui facio istuc . . ." *Confessions* Books I–IV, edited Gillian Clark (Cambridge: Cambridge University Press, 1995). All subsequent Latin citations from Books II–IV are taken from this edition.

33. *Confessions*, IV. ix (14).

"Hoc est quod diligitur in amicis, et sic diligitur ut rea sibi sit humana conscientia si non amauerit redamantem aut si amantem non redamauerit . . . hinc ille luctus si quis moriatur, et tenebrae dolorum et uersa dulcedine in amaritudinem cor madidum et ex amissa uita morientium mors uiuentium."

34. See *Confessions* IX.iii (6).

35. WD, 121.

"Écrire et la perte; mais la perte sans don (un don sans contrepartie) risque toujours d'être une perte apaisante qui apporte la sécurité. C'est pourquoi il n'y a sans doute pas de discours amoureux, sinon de l'amour dans son absence, «vécu» dans la perte, le vieillissement, c'est-à-dire la mort." ED, 186.

36. *Friendship*, 171. Here, interestingly, Blanchot is writing of Klossowski.

"La discrétion—la réserve—est le lieu de la littérature. Le chemin le plus court d'un point à un autre est littérairement l'oblique ou l'asymptote. Qui parle directement ne parle pas ou parle mensongèrement, par conséquent sans autre direction que la perte de toute droiture. La rapport juste au monde est le détour, et ce détour n'est juste que s'il se maintient, dans l'écart et la distance, comme mouvement pur de se détourner." *L'Amitié*, 194.

37. WD, 105.

". . . au lieu de l'ultimité, brûlure inconsumable d'où s'exclut tout achèvement, tout accomplissement dans une présence. Attente infini comme inattendue. Oubli, souvenir de l'immémorial, sans mémoire." ED, 163.

38. Roland Barthes, *A lover's discourse*, translated by Richard Howard (NY: Hill and Wang, 1978), 107. Hereafter, LD.

"Le point le plus sensible de ce deuil n'est-il pas qu'il me faut *perdre un langage*— le langage amoureux? Fini les «Je t'aime»." *Fragments d'un discours amoureux* (Paris: Éditions du seuil, 1977), 124. Hereafter, FDA.

39. LD, 14–15.

"Cette absence bien supportée, elle n'est rien d'autre que l'oubli. Je suis, par intermittence, infidèle. C'est la condition de ma survie; car, si je n'oubliais pas, je mourrais. L'amoureux qui n'oublie pas *quelquefois*, meurt par excès, fatigue et tension de mémoire . . ." FDA, 20.

40. LD, 15.

"De cet oubli, très vite, je me réveille. Hâtivement, je mets en place un mémoire. . . ." FDA, 21.

41. LD, 30.

". . . elle est la crainte d'un deuil qui a déjà eu lieu, dès l'origine de l'amour . . ." FDA, 38.

42. IC, 192–93.

"Déjà les Anciens avaient pressenti que Léthé n'est pas seulement l'envers d'Aléthéia, son ombre, la puissance négative dont nous déliverait le savoir qui se rappelle: Léthé est aussi le compagnon d'Éros, l'éveil propre au sommeil, cela, l'écart, dont il n'y a pas donc sans traces, s'effaçant en toutes traces et qui pourtant—il faut en avancer fautivement l'expression—s'annonce encore, se désigne déjà dans le manque à écrire dont l'écriture—ce jeu insensé—se souvient hors mémoire comme sa limite ou de son illégitimité toujours préalable." EI, 288.

43. Eliot, "East Coker," from Four Quartets, V.

44. TBR 1, 48.

"Dieu parle dans l'oubli. Sa parole est oubli." LR, 70.

45. TBR 1, 108–09.

"Dieu est seul à ne point parle où Il parle; c'est pourquoi Dieu ne peut être que le silence où s'épuise toute parole; mais, alors, si Dieu est silence, quelle est cette parole divine que nous entendons? Si Dieu est absence, quel est ce livre divin que nous commentons? Et quel est ce destin d'homme qui se confondrait avec ceui de la parole tue de nos livres? Nul destin, à ce qui n' pas vu le jour. Nul avenir, à ce qui est sans existence." LR, 145.

46. IE, 36.

"Oubli de tout. Profonde descente dans la nuit de l'existence. Supplication infinie de l'ignorance, se noyer d'angoisse. Se glisser au-dessus de l'abîme et dans l'obscurité achevée en éprouver l'horreur. Trembler, désepérer, dans le froid de la solitude, dans le silence éternel de l'homme (sottise de toute phrase, illusoires réponses des phrases, seul le silence insensé de la nuit répond). Le mot «Dieu,» s'en être servi pour atteindre le fond de la solitude, mais ne plus savoir, entendre sa voix. . . . Dieu dernier mot voulant dire que tout mot, un peu plus loin manquera . . ." L'EI, 49.

47. Jean-Luc Nancy, "Of divine places," in The inoperative community, translated by Peter Connor, Lisa Garbus, Michael Holland, and Simona Sawhney (Minneapolis: University of Minnesota Press, 1991), 128.

"Il y a le dieu qui s'approche de l'homme, jusqu'à le toucher, et il y a le dieu qui s'éloigne de lui, jusqu'à le délaisser infiniment. Les deux sont le même: le dieu qui touche l'homme le touche pour le laisser à lui-même, non pour le prendre ni pour le retenir." "Des lieux divins," in *Qu'est-ce que Dieu? Philosophie/ Théologie. Hommage à l'abbé Daniel Coppieters de Gibson (1929–1983)* (Brussels: Publications des Facultés Univesitaires Saint-Louis, 1985), 560.

48. Confessions X.xix (28)

"neque enim omni modo adhuc obliti sumus, quod vel oblitos nos esse meminimus. hoc ergo nec amissum quaerere poterimus, quod omnino obliti fuerimus."

49. LBUS, 16.

"L'oubli est, dans tout souvenir, le souvenir mort-né qui afflige la mémoire." PLSHS, 22.

50. PN, 131.

"L'extérieur n'est pas le lointain." SMB, 14.

51. Elaine Pagels, The Gnostic gospels (NY: Random House, 1979), 50. Pagels refers here to the anti-Gnostic Iranaeus, *Libros quinque adversus haereses*, I.13.6 and I.13.2. In his zeal to counter Valentinus, Iranaueus became a valuable preserver of his thought.

52. Turner, 71.

53. *New international bible*, John 1:17.

54. *New international bible*, Paul, Letter to the Romans, 5:20–21.

55. Wayne Meeks, editor, *The Writings of St. Paul*, annotated text and criticism (New York: W.W. Norton and Co., 1972), 216.

56. Augustine, "On Grace and Free Will," chapter xxiv, in Meeks, 225.

57. *New international bible*, Paul, Romans 11:6.

58. *New international bible*, Paul, Ephesians 2.8–10, my emphasis.

59. Augustine, "On Grace and Free will," ch. xliii, in Meeks, 233.

60. Hollywood, 154.

61. SNB, 25.

"La loi tue. La mort est toujours horizon de la loi: si tu fais cela, tu mourras. Elle tue celui qui ne l'observe pas, et l'observer, c'est aussi déjà mourir, mourir à toutes les possibilités . . ." PAD, 38.

62. SNB, 25.

"La grâce ne sauve pas de la mort, mais elle efface la condamnation mortelle en faisant du *saltus mortalis*—l'élan sans retenue et sans précaution—le mouvement insouciant qui ne se soucie ni de condamnation ni de salut, étant le don qui ne pèse et ne se pèse, don de la légèreté, don toujours léger." PAD, 38–39.

63. Nancy, "Of divine places," 135.

"Face à face, mais sans plus se voir désormais, les dieux et les hommes sont abandonnés à l'écriture." "Des lieux divins," 569.

64. *New international bible*, Exodus 20:2–17.

65. *New international bible*, Exodus 20:24.

66. *New international bible*, Exodus 31:18; 32:15–16.

67. *New international bible*, Exodus 34:4, 34:27–28.

68. *New international bible*, Genesis 11:1–9.

69. Shapiro, Marianne, *De vulgari eloquentia: Dante's book of Exile* (Lincoln: University of Nebraska Press, 1990), 24.

70. Shapiro, 1990, 50.

71. Hill, MBEC, 127. Note cites *The Heidegger controversy: a critical reader*, edited by Richard Wolin, 107, translation modified by Hill.

$\mathcal{W}$orks cited

Anselm, Saint. *Proslogion*. bilingual edition, translated and introduced by M. J. Charlesworth. Notre Dame, IL: Notre Dame University Press, 1979.

Aquinas, St. Thomas. *Summa Theologiae*. translated by the Fathers of the English Dominican Province. NY: Benzinger Brothers, 1925.

Aristotle. *Metaphysics*. translated by Richard Hope. Ann Arbor: University of Michigan Press, 1960.

Artaud, Antonin. *The Artaud anthology*. edited by Jack Hirschman, various translators. San Francisco: City Lights Books, 1965, from: *L'Ombilic des Limbes*, Paris: Gallimard, 1968.

Augustine, Saint. *Confessions*. translated by Henry Chadwick. New York: Oxford University Press, 1991. my sources for original text: *St. Augustine's confessions, with an English translation*. volume 2. William Watts. New York: G. P. Putnam's Sons, 1931; *Confessions Books I–IV*. edited Gillian Clark. Cambridge: Cambridge University Press, 1995.

————. *The teacher*. in *St. Augustine: The greatness of the soul* and *The teacher*, translated by Joseph M. Colleran, Westminster, MD: The Newman Press, 1950.

Barthes, Roland. *A lover's discourse*. translated by Richard Howard. NY: Hill and Wang, 1978, from: *Fragments d'un discours amoureux*, Paris: Éditions du seuil, 1977.

Bataille, Georges. *Erotism: death and sensuality*. translated by Mary Dalwood. San Francisco: City Lights Books, 1986, from: *L'Erotisme*. Paris: Éditions de Minuit. 1957.

————. *Guilty*. translated by Bruce Boone. Venice, CA: Lapis Press, 1988, from: *Le coupable*. Paris: Éditions Gallimard, 1961.

————. *Inner experience*. translated by Leslie Ann Boldt. Albany: SUNY Press, 1988, from: *L'Experience interieure*. Paris: Éditions Gallimard, 1954.

————. *Theory of religion*. translated by Robert Hurley. New York: Zone Books, 1989, from: *Théorie de la religion*. Paris: Éditions Gallimard, 1973.

————. *Visions of excess: selected writings 1927–1939*. (posthumous collection) translated by Allen Stoekel, with Carl R. Lovitt and Donald M. Leslie, Jr. Minneapolis: University of Minnesota Press, 1985.

Baudrillard, Jean. *Seduction*. translated by Brian Singer. New York: St. Martin's Press, 1990, from: *De la séduction*. Paris: Éditions Galilée, 1979.

Biale, David. *Gershom Scholem: Kabbalah and counter-history*. Cambridge, MA: Harvard University Press, 1982.

——. "Jewish Mysticism in the Sixteenth Century." In *Medieval Mystics*. edited by Paul Szarmach. Albany: SUNY Press, 1984.

Blanchot, Maurice. *Awaiting oblivion*. translated by John Gregg. Lincoln, NB: University of Nebraska Press, 1997, from: *L'attente l'oubli*. Paris: Gallimard, 1962.

——. *Friendship*. translated by Elizabeth Rottenberg. Stanford: Stanford University Press, 1997, from: *L'Amitié*. Paris: Gallimard, 1971.

——. *The infinite conversation*. translated by Susan Hanson. Minneapolis: University of Minnesota Press, 1993, from: *L'Entretien infini*. Paris: Éditions Gallimard, 1969.

——. *The space of literature*. translated by Ann Smock. Lincoln: University of Nebraska Press, 1982, from: *L'espace litéraire*. Paris: Éditions Gallimard, 1955.

——. *The step not beyond*. translated by Lycette Nelson. Albany: SUNY Press, 1992, from: *Le pas au-delà*. Paris: Éditions Gallimard, 1973.

——. *The Writing of the disaster*. translated by Ann Smock. Lincoln: University of Nebraska Press, 1986, from: *L'écriture du désastre*. Paris: Éditions Gallimard, 1980.

Boldt-Irons, Leslie Anne, editor. *On Bataille: critical essays*. Albany: SUNY Press, 1988.

Caputo, John. *The prayers and tears of Jacques Derrida: religion without religion*. Bloomington: Indiana University Press, 1997.

Celan, Paul. *Breathturn*. 1967. bilingual edition. translated by Pierre Joris. Los Angeles: Sun and Moon Press, 1995.

——. *Paul Celan, collected prose*. translated by Rosmarie Waldrop. Riverdale-on-Hudson, NY: Sheep Meadow Press, 1986, from: *Paul Celan: Der Meridian und andere Prosa*, Frankfurt: Suhrkamp, 1988.

——. *Poems of Paul Celan*. bilingual edition. translated by Michael Hamburger. NY: Persea Books, 1988.

Constantine, David. *Hölderlin*. Oxford: Clarendon Press, 1988.

Deleuze, Gilles. *Coldness and cruelty*. translated by Jean McNeil. New York: Zone Books, 1989, from: *Présentation de Sacher-Masoch: le Froid et le Cruel*. Paris: Éditions de Minuit, 1967.

Derrida, Jacques. *Sauf le nom*, in *On the name*, edited Thomas Dutoit. Stanford: Stanford University Press, 1995, from: *Sauf le nom*, Paris: Éditions Galilée, 1993, 61.

Eckhart, Meister Johannes. *The best of Meister Eckhart*. Edited by Halcyon Backhouse. New York: Crossroad Publishing, 1995.

——. *Selected writings*. Edited and translated by Oliver Davies. New York: Penguin Books, 1994, from:*Meister Eckhart: Die deutschen und lateinischen Werke, dritter*

Band, Stuttgart: W. Kohlhammer, three volumes, 1971–1976, and: F. Jostes, ed., *Meister Eckhart und seine Jünger: ungedruckte zur Geschichte der deutschen Mystik*, De Gruyter, 1972.

Eliade, Mircea. *The sacred and the profane*. translated by Willard R. Trask. NY: Harcourt Brace Jovanovich, 1959.

Eliot, Thomas Stearns. *Four quartets*. NY: Harcourt Brace Jovanovich, 1943.

———. *Selected poems*. NY: Harcourt Brace Jovanovich, 1936.

Fioretos, Aris, editor. *Word traces: readings of Paul Celan*. Baltimore: Johns Hopkins University Press, 1994.

Förster, Eckart. *The course of remembrance and other essays on Hölderlin*, edited by Dieter Henrich. Stanford: Stanford Univerity Press, 1997.

Foucault, Michel. *Language countermemory practice*. edited and translated by Donald F. Bouchard and Sherry Simon. Ithaca: Cornell University Press, 1977. originals include: "Preface à transgression," *Critique*, 195–96, 1963.

———. *Madness and civilization*. translator unnamed. London: Routledge, 1989, from: *Folie et deraison*, Paris: Plon, 1971.

———. *Thought from the outside*. in *Foucault/ Blanchot*. translated by Jeffrey Mehlman and Brian Massumi. NY: Zone Books, 1990, from: *La pensée du dehors, Critique*, 229, 1966.

Gill, Carolyn Bailey, editor. *Maurice Blanchot: the demand of writing*. London: Routledge, 1996.

Gould, Eric, editor. *The sin of the book: Edmond Jabès*. Lincoln, NB: University of Nebraska Press, 1985.

Haar, Michel. "Nietzsche and metaphysical language." in *The new Nietzsche*. edited by David Allison. Cambridge: MIT Press, 1985.

Heidegger, Martin. *Basic Writings*. edited David Farrell Krell. NY: Harper and Row, 1977, from *Was heißt Denken?* Tübingen: Max Niemeyer, 1971. and: *Wegmarken*. Frankfurt: Vittorio Klostermann, 1967.

Hill, Leslie. *Maurice Blanchot: extreme contemporary*. NY: Routledge, 1997.

Hölderlin, Friedrich. *Friedrich Hölderlin: poems and fragments*. bilingual edition . translated by Michael Hamburger. Ann Arbor: University of Michigan Press, 1968.

Holland, Michael, editor. *The Blanchot reader*. Oxford: Blackwell, 1995.

Holthusen, Hans Egon. *Rainer Maria Rilke: a study of his later poetry*. Translated by J. P. Stern. New Haven: Yale, 1952.

Holy Bible: New international version. various authors. NY: Harper Paperbacks, 1984.

Jabès, Edmond. *The book of resemblances*. translated by Rosmarie Waldrop. Hanover and London: Wesleyan University Press, 1991, from: *Le livre des resemblances, L'inefaçable L'inaperçu*. Paris: Gallimard, 1980.

———. *The little book of unsuspected subversion*. translated by Rosmarie Waldrop. Stanford: Stanford University Press, 1996, from: *Le petit livre de subversion hors de soupçon*. Paris: Gallimard, 1982.

Klossowski, Pierre. *Nietzsche and the vicious circle*. translated by Daniel W. Smith. Chicago: University of Chicago Press, 1997, from: *Nietzsche et le cercle vicieux*, Paris: Mercure de France, 1969.

Levinas, Emmanuel. *Proper names*. translated by Michael B. Smith. Stanford: Stanford University Press, 1996, from: *Noms propre*, Paris: Fata Morgana, 1976, and: *Sur Maurice Blanchot*, Paris: Fata Morgana, 1975.

Manchester, Peter. "The religious experience of time and eternity," in A. H. Armstrong, editor, *Classical Mediterranean spirituality*, NY: Crossroad, 1980.

Meeks, Wayne, editor. *The Writings of St. Paul, annotated text and criticism*. New York: W.W. Norton and Co., 1972.

Nancy, Jean-Luc. "Of divine places." in *The inoperative community*. edited by Peter Connor. Minneapolis: University of Minnesota Press, 1991, from: "Des lieux divins," in *Q'est-ce que Dieu?* Brussels: Publications des Facultés Universitaires Saint-Louis, 1985.

Niebylski, Dianna C. *The poem on the edge of the world: the limits of language and the uses of silence in the poetry of Malarmé, Rilke, and Vallejo*. NY: Peter Lang, 1993.

Nietzsche, Friedrich. *The gay science*. translated by Walter Kaufmann. New York: Vintage Books, 1974, from: *Die Fröliche Wissenschaft*, in *Werke II*. Frankfurt: Ullstein, 1984.

———. *The Will to power*, translated by Walter Kaufmann and R. J. Hollingdale, New York: Vintage Books, 1968, from: *Der Wille zur Macht*, Leipzig: Alfred Kröner Verlag, 1928.

Pagels, Elaine. *The Gnostic gospels*. New York: Random House, 1979.

Plato. *The Meno*, in *The collected dialogues of Plato*, edited by Edith Hamilton and Huntington Cairns. Princeton: Princeton University Press, 1961.

———. *Phaedrus*, translated by Alexander Nehamas and Paul Woodruff. Indianapolis: Hackett Publishing, 1995.

———. *Republic*, in *The collected dialogues of Plato*.

Plotinus. *Enneads*. translated by Stephen Mackenna. NY: Penguin Books, 1991.

Rilke, Rainer Maria. *Rainer Maria Rilke: new poems*. bilingual edition. translated by Edward Snow. New York: Farrar, Strauss and Giroux, 1984.

———. *The selected poetry of Rainer Maria Rilke*. bilingual edition. translated by Stephen Mitchell. New York: Vintage Books, 1989.

Rosenthal, Bianca. *Pathways to Paul Celan: A history of critical responses as a chorus of discordant voices*, New York: Peter Lang Publishing, 1995.

Scholem, Gershom. *The Messianic idea in Judaism and other essays on Jewish spirituality*. New York: Schocken Books, 1971.

Schopenhauer, Arthur. *The will to live*. edited and translated by Richard Taylor. New York: Anchor Books, 1962.

Shapiro, Marianne. *De vulgari eloquentia: Dante's book of exile*. Lincoln, NB: University of Nebraska Press, 1990.

Tilley, Maureen, and Susan Ross, editors. *Broken and whole*. Lanham, MD: University Press of America, 1995.

Wittgenstein, Ludwig. *Tractatus logico-philosophicus*. bilingual edition. translated by C. K. Ogden. London: Routledge and Kegan Paul, 1922, from: *Logische-philosophische Abhandlung*, in same edition.

Index

absence, 5, 23, 24, 35, 49, 68, 110;
Augustine and, 74; Blanchot and,
19; Celan and, 54; of God, 12–16,
49, 50, 51, 52, 62, 65, 97, 105; God
as, 108; Jabès and, 51–52; language
of, 107; memory and, 100, 105, 106;
presence and, 79; space and, 99–100;
of time, 19, 113
Adam, 59
amnesia, 95, 96, 97
anamnesis, 8, 95, 97
Anselm, Saint, 6
apophatic theology, 3, 5, 12, 97
Aristotle, 86
art, 1, 98, 99
Artaud, Antonin, 44–45; quoted, 2, 73
"As on holiday" (Hölderlin), 63
atemporality, 2, 24, 51, 75, 79, 102. *See
also* temporality
Atemwende, 58
atheism, 5
Augustine, Saint, 10, 16–17, 51, 71–80,
97, 102, 106, 112; Eckhart and, 81,
82, 87, 88, 89; forgetfulness and, 17,
59, 109; on law and grace, 110–11;
memory and, 26, 100, 107, 108
Auschwitz, 54, 55, 60
Awaiting oblivion (Blanchot), 101, 104

Babel, 112
Barthes, Roland, 107
Bataille, Georges, 5, 13, 16, 28–29,
33–45, 65, 81, 83, 90, 97, 102, 104;

art and, 99; Blanchot's writings about,
27, 30, 31; desire and, 53; eroticism
and, 4; eternal recurrence and, 9; forgetfulness and, 50, 109; fragmentation
and, 53; language and, 104; quoted,
26, 47; unknowing and, 3, 90; violence and, 25; writing and, 22
Baudrillard, Jean, 4
Baudry, Jean-Luis, 41–42
Being, 11–12, 83, 88, 96
Biale, David, 13, 15
Blanchot, Maurice, 13, 15, 17–31, 51,
52–53, 59, 85, 88, 96, 97, 102, 103,
107, 113; art and, 99; conversation
and, 55, 56; eternal return and, 8;
forgetfulness and, 50, 98, 101, 104;
fragmentation and, 53; grace and,
111; language and, 45; literature and,
106; madness and, 48; outside and, 3,
18, 27, 28–31; philosophy and, 5;
quoted, 11, 53, 59, 65, 87, 111;
sacred and, 83; spaces and, 99; violence and, 25, 36; withdrawal of gods
and, 14, 15; writing and, 34
"Bonaparte" (Hölderlin), 60

Caputo, John, 83
Catherine of Siena, 81
Celan, Paul, 7, 16, 48, 53–59, 63, 96;
Hölderlin's influence on, 59; quoted,
12, 19, 33
Christ, 99, 110; Hölderlin and, 61; New
Testament, 59. *See also* God

165